AMERICAN WOMEN

images and realities

AMERICAN WOMEN
Images and Realities

Advisory Editors
ANNETTE K. BAXTER
LEON STEIN

A Note About This Volume

At 50, Boston-born Gamaliel Bradford (1863-1932) won literary renown with a biography of Robert E. Lee. Between 1917 and 1932 he produced thirteen additional volumes of "psychographs," most successfully as collections of short sketches with penetrating interpretations of prosaic data that reveal the spirit of his subjects. "Wives" focuses on women who often in all but fame, were the equals of their husbands and fathers—Abraham Lincoln, Benedict Arnold, Aaron Burr, James Madison, Jefferson Davis, Benjamin Butler and James G. Blaine—whose roles in history rescued them from obscurity.

WIVES

BY

GAMALIEL BRADFORD

ARNO PRESS

A New York Times Company

New York • 1972

- - - - - - - - - - - - - -

Library of Congress Cataloging in Publication Data

Bradford, Gamaliel, 1863-1932.
   Wives.

   (American women: images and realities)
   1. Women in the United States--Biography.
I. Title. II. Series.
CT3260.B743 1972   920.7'2   72-2591
ISBN 0-405-04448-8

WIVES

MRS. ABRAHAM LINCOLN

WIVES

BY

GAMALIEL BRADFORD

*Author of "Bare Souls," "The Soul of Samuel
Pepys," "Damaged Souls," etc.*

WITH ILLUSTRATIONS

NEW YORK AND LONDON

HARPER & BROTHERS

PUBLISHERS

WIVES

L-Z

TO
H. F. B.

CONTENTS

ILLUSTRATIONS

PREFACE

IN a previous volume, entitled "Portraits of American Women," I discussed a group of women who were mainly notable for their own achievements, quite independent of the other sex. Five of them were unmarried. Two, Mrs. Ripley and Mrs. Stowe, had husbands, but they were rather incidental. Mrs. President Adams alone owed her reputation to her marriage, though she had quite enough in her own character and intelligence to justify it. With this book the case is different, and the women portrayed in it would probably have lived quiet, utterly unknown lives except for their masculine connections, unless Sarah Butler might have succeeded in making a name for herself on the stage. Theodosia Burr owes her historical position to her father, although she was a wife and an interesting one, and the remaining six to their husbands. Yet it is curious that, in every instance except that of Mrs. Lincoln, one gets an indefinable sense of full equality with the husband, and in one or two instances a sense of decided superiority. One is reminded of the striking passage in which Henry Adams insists to some of his distinguished friends that the American woman is distinctly superior to the American man: " 'Has not my sister here more sense than my brother Brooks? Is not Bessie worth two of Bay [Lodge]? Wouldn't we all elect Mrs. Lodge Senator against Cabot? Would the President have a ghost of a chance if Mrs. Roosevelt ran against him? Do you want to stop at the Embassy, on your way home, and ask which would run it best—Herbert or his wife?' The men laughed a little—not much. Each probably made allowance for his own wife as an unusually superior woman. Some one afterward remarked that these half dozen women were not a fair average. Adams replied that the half dozen men were above all possible average; he could not lay his hands on another half dozen their equals." The brilliant author of the *Education* is here indulging, to some extent, in his habitual rhetoric. All the same, it must be admitted that the women analyzed in these pages assist his contention most interestingly.

I must acknowledge my debt for constant and varied helpfulness to the Librarian of the Boston Athenæum and his efficient staff. The authorities of the Massachusetts Historical Society, the Boston Public Library, and the Harvard College Library have granted me exceptional favors. I am under obligations to an unusually long list of correspondents. In my investigations for Mrs. Lincoln I have received valuable aid from Rev. William E. Barton, Mr. Nicholas Vachel Lindsay, Professor N. W. Stephenson, Miss Mary E. Humphrey, Mrs. Francis P. Ide. For Mrs. Davis, Miss Susan B. Harrison, the able Curator of the Confederate Museum in Richmond, has allowed me the use of material from the Jefferson Hayes Davis collection and has herself most kindly examined that material and made copies. A similar service has been performed by Dr. Douglas Freeman. Professor Stephenson has assisted me also in my study of Mrs. Davis, and I am especially indebted to Mr. Matthew Page Andrews, Professor Pierce Butler, and Professor Walter L. Fleming, also to Miss Jennie P. Buford. Through the friendly offices of Mr. C. K. Bolton, Mrs. Laura E. Richards, and Miss Mary C. Sawyer I have obtained much important information regarding Mrs. Blaine from Chief-Justice L. C. Cornish, Mr. Samuel Manley, Mr. Norman L. Bassett, Mr. Edward Nelson Dingley, Mr. Louis Addison Dent, Mrs. John Cummings, Mrs. Eugene Hale. To all these I wish to express my most appreciative thanks.

GAMALIEL BRADFORD

Wellesley Hills, Massachusetts.

xiii

I
CONFESSIONS OF A BIOGRAPHER

Wives of great men all remind us,
     We can make our lives sublime.

LONGFELLOW (slightly emended)

We women were the last of God's works: you
feel that He was tired.

FRENCH COMEDY

WIVES

CONFESSIONS OF A BIOGRAPHER

BIOGRAPHY is much in fashion at present. The brilliant and fascinating studies of Mr. Strachey have been accompanied and followed by all kinds of biographical efforts, some superficial and gossipy, some heavily documented and tedious, some winging their way gayly through a current publicity and popularity, some treated with respect and stowed safely on the shelf, to afford curious information to a posterity which may, or may not, be too busy to look for it. But nearly everything biographical finds readers, much of it many readers; and it almost seems as if even the horde and herd of devourers of fiction was partially sated with its favorite diet and was turning instinctively to an order of reading which at least professes to be somewhat more veracious. Not that fiction also does not fundamentally depend upon human truth. So far as it is based upon such truth it really holds readers, and they soon turn from it indifferently when such truth is far away. Still, there is a charm about the actual lives of men and women, people who have had known names, who have walked the solid earth with solid tread, who have suffered and struggled and hoped and loved and lied and laughed as we have. Such is the matter of biography, and, being made of such stuff, it will always have the most vivid appeal of any form of serious literature.

People are apt to think that biography is also an easy form of literature to write. A man is born and grows up and marries—or not—and acts and speaks and dies. All you have to do is to pick up the facts and set them down. It sounds simple enough; so that people write biographies who never write anything else and obviously never could. All the same, there are difficulties. Perhaps one who has wrestled with these for a considerable number of years and has found them so immense that he is hopelessly discontented with his results, may be pardoned for dwelling upon a few of them.

To begin with, there is the purely artistic difficulty. The biography must be made interesting, must be made beautiful, must be a well composed, designed, combined, and finished performance. It is not enough to string facts together in a disordered multiplicity. The biographer must select, weigh, discard. He must omit nothing that is

4

essential to the understanding and estimating of his subject; he must introduce nothing that distracts. He must make a clear, direct, vivid narrative, one that is rich with suggested background of antecedent, connection, and consequence, yet is not hampered or clogged by the irrelevant episodes and characters that are perpetually teasing and tempting him aside. It is no easy matter to combine veracity and vivacity. As Mr. Strachey, whose success is so notable, admirably says: "The most delicate and humane of all the branches of the art of writing has been relegated to the journeymen of letters; we do not realize that it is perhaps as difficult to write a good life as to live one."

But this difficulty of artistic handling is the smallest part of a biographer's troubles, so small that he must leave it to the providence of God, knowing that if Heaven has not endowed him with an instinctive gift for it, he has simply got into the wrong business. There are other matters to which he has to give early and undivided attention, if he is to take care of them properly.

First, there are what we may call the subjective difficulties, those that are inherent in the mind and temper of the writer himself. It is customary to speak of partial and impartial biographies. There are no impartial biographies, or histories, either;

there are only some that are less partial than others. The man does not exist who can write on any subject without preconception, without *postconception*, with a complete absence of personal bias which sways him to one judgment or another. In fact, the best biographies are apt to be those that are written with a considerable amount of bias, for or against. To begin with, there are the general prejudices of race, creed, politics, social training and position, which no man ever escapes entirely. You may recognize these, you may endeavor to discount them; in that case the result is, as often as not, that you go to the other extreme in the effort to be perfectly fair. If one may cite oneself, I have been struggling for years now to arrive at an impartial estimate of Benjamin F. Butler. Before I studied him at all, my mind was so inrooted and enwrapped with prejudices in regard to him, that it seemed impossible ever to disentangle it. I don't know that I have disentangled it. I may have reacted against the original prejudice too much. In any event, the result, when I came to portray him, did not satisfy his enemies or his friends, and certainly not me.

Again, apart from these original preconceptions, any biographer who is at all sensitive will quickly arrive at a personal feeling about his subject.

which is almost sure to distort the abstract justice of his conclusions. Our lives are made up of likes and dislikes, which we cannot explain, and exactly these instinctive attractions and repulsions are almost certain to play the deuce with biography. If I may again illustrate personally, I knew nothing of Charles Sumner before I came to write of him, had no established prejudice, unless very mildly in favor. But as soon as I got into his soul—if he had one—he irritated me. I knew that he was an excellent man, a man of large philanthropy and solid patriotism. I tried to emphasize these things. I did emphasize them. All the same, he irritated me, and the irritation got into my portrait. So with Frances Willard. She was a splendid woman, only I could not bear her, would have walked miles to avoid meeting her, and that got into my portrait, too. But there was Aaron Burr, one of the most vicious, dangerous, disreputable figures in American history. Yet most people loved Aaron Burr, especially most women, and so did I. I couldn't help it. And even while I portrayed his weaknesses as vividly as I knew how, I was apologizing for them against my will.

Still another subjective element that works against impartiality is the natural instinct of the writer to heighten lights and shadows merely for

7

artistic effect. Whether you like the figure you are drawing or dislike it, you are tempted to emphasize good and bad qualities beyond the truth, simply to impress the reader and make a telling picture. Everyone appreciates how intensely this temptation beset Macaulay, and how prone he was to yield to it. But no biographer escapes it altogether. Even the judicious and controlled Sainte-Beuve complains bitterly that exaggeration is the perpetual danger. It is so easy to use a strong adjective unqualified, so easy to make a white virtue out of a casual complacency, or to turn a regretted and forgotten error into a blasting sin.

So much for the difficulties inherent in the writer himself. There are others in the man written about, quite as serious and perhaps even more subtle and perplexing. Evidently little biography is written from direct personal knowledge of the subject himself, and that little is rarely of the most satisfactory sort. Biographers in general have to rely mainly upon documents, either printed or manuscript. Printed material can never be relied upon with entire assurance. What was printed before the middle of the nineteenth century can rarely be relied upon with any assurance at all. The liberties taken by older editors in the reproduction of historical manuscripts are enough to shake one's confidence in human nature, if one ever had any. Yet the original manuscripts have often been destroyed and in almost all cases are difficult to consult and to deal with.

But suppose we have an abundance of material; and we usually have too great an abundance of it, such as it is. This material divides into what the man tells us of himself, either in speech or in writing, and what is told of him by others. The estimate of others is often interesting and valuable, always taking into account the personal idiosyncrasy of the reporter, his greater or less degree of intimacy with the subject, his power of impartial observation, and his natural sympathy or repulsion for the temperament discussed. The trouble with these external witnesses is that they rarely agree and often actually contradict each other, and then what is a puzzled biographer to do? Take Lincoln: in the enormous mass of testimony that comes to us about him there are verdicts of equally good judges that conflict entirely. Is one to reject both, or accept both and make some awkward endeavor to reconcile them? So with Woodrow Wilson and the numerous documents that are daily appearing from those who have known him intimately. From one set we should get an entirely different picture of the man from that given by the other. It requires fine tact and thoughtful balancing to achieve a composite result that will do injustice to neither side.

When we come to a man's testimony about himself, we have to deal either with spoken words recorded by others, or with his own actual writing. The first source of information is obviously of great importance, but must be used with extreme caution. History and biography are full of quoted sayings, and these are often so pregnant and suggestive that the temptation to employ them is almost irresistible. Yet we must remember that they are seldom taken down on the spot, are usually recorded from memory a considerable time after they were uttered, and often by persons whose memory is anything but trained to exactitude. It is rare that any of us can reproduce his own words after a few hours' interval, rare indeed that we can reproduce another's. Yet writers of diaries and letters will set down long conversations in quotation marks, and these are repeated and handed on in history as an exact record of the utterance of celebrated persons, when the said celebrated persons would probably disown a large part of them in disgust. The Goncourts were most carefully trained and disciplined observers and listeners; yet Renan and others declared that their

10

conversations, as recorded in the Goncourts' Journal, belied them utterly.

When we come to what a man has himself actually written, we are on surer ground. At least we know what he said. Then comes the question of what he meant to say, whether he is deliberately deceiving us, whether he was unconsciously deceiving himself, and the puzzle becomes more complex than ever, and we are quite at sea again. What is perhaps most interesting of all is the varying instinct of self-revelation in different persons. Take the two extremes. Take a writer like Pepys, who has an actual genius for turning his soul inside out, whose every page and almost every phrase is laden with spiritual significance. And then take a man like General Lee, of far profounder and infinitely more interesting nature than Pepys, but a man who instinctively keeps all the secrets of his heart hid away so deeply that it is only by the most patient search and the most watchful observation that you can get a glimpse of it at all. Take two other men of great intellectual power and great prominence in the world's history, Voltaire and Thomas Jefferson. Both were vast letter-writers, perhaps the greatest whose correspondence has been preserved to us, Voltaire leaving some ten thousand letters, and Jefferson nearer twenty.

11

Voltaire's letters, even the most insignificant, glitter and sparkle with life, the life of Voltaire; Jefferson's are dull, roll on with a wide, unchecked garrulity, but have very rarely any revelation of the man's soul.

So much for the material, and I hope I have made sufficiently plain what the biographer's difficulties are in dealing with the substance of his work. But even when the material is given, there remains the hardest part of the task, that of interpretation. It is little to know the facts, although we never do know them; we must also know what they mean. In other words, the real object of the biographer, all that deeply and permanently interests him, is the analysis and synthesis of his subject's character. What is character? Simply the sum of qualities. And what are qualities? So far as the external observer is concerned, they are the generalization of habits of speech and action. An honest man is one who does honest things. A mean man is one who does mean things. A strenuous man is one who does strenuous things. Now, as we all, at some time or other, do things honest and dishonest, mean and generous, strenuous and indolent, and so on without end, it will readily be seen how immensely difficult is the task of determining what tendency is sufficiently fixed to constitute a quality. It is

12

this complication, this variance, this perpetual shift and change in the complexion of men's souls, largely, that causes the untruth of history, that keeps the unthinking perpetually at odds over the solidity of greatness, that makes us forever unable to determine the enduring worth of glory or the substantial permanence of human example. Though all his materials were assured and guaranteed, were fixed and solid and reliable, as they never are, the biographer would have no confidence in his own work or in that of others, because between the material and the result there comes always this insuperable difficulty of the interpretation which no perseverance, no ingenuity, no insight can ever make binding or absolute.

In view of all these complicated troubles it might naturally be supposed that the biographer would give up. But he cannot. The fascination of his task is incomparable and grows with his deeper comprehension of its growing difficulty. Of all the studies of the world there is none more absorbing than this of the individual soul. The fascination of writers and readers both depends upon the fact that they themselves are individual souls, and this grave and subtle complexity, which affects the men and women they read about, affects themselves also. We must study human souls in order to live. Our world is made up of them, and we cannot take a step or draw a breath without some dependence upon their interactions and reactions. Every living human being is a biographer from childhood, in that he perpetually studies the souls of those about him, detects with keen and curious thought the resemblances and differences between those souls and that still more present and puzzling entity, his own, and weighs with the most anxious care the bearing and effect of others' thoughts and actions upon his own life. It is this immediate personal concern that accounts for our passionate interest in formal biography. The interest is natural and human and enduring; it can never die. Only, it must be remembered that no biography is to be accepted as final. At least, that is the conclusion of one humble and insignificant biographer as to his own work, and his haunting suspicion as to the work of others.

II

MRS. ABRAHAM LINCOLN

CHRONOLOGY

Mary Todd Lincoln.
Born, Lexington, Kentucky, December 13, 1818.
Educated in Kentucky and lived there till 1839.
Married Lincoln, November 4, 1842.
Son Willie died, 1862.
Lincoln assassinated, April 14, 1865.
Son Tad died, 1871.
Died, July 16, 1882.

MRS. ABRAHAM LINCOLN

I

KINGS and princes are in the habit of selecting their wives, or having them selected, with a view to the exalted station they are destined to occupy. Presidents of the United States usually marry young, like other men, and do not arrive at the White House until they are old, and sometimes they bring with them partners not wholly adapted to such a conspicuous career. The complication in Lincoln's case is peculiar. A brilliant but uncouth and almost grotesque lawyer and politician from the backwoods, with no inherited social position or distinction, marries a showy, popular belle, who considers herself an aristocrat in the limited circle which is all she knows, and feels that she is condescending vastly in accepting the husband whose only asset is an extremely nebulous future. Then the husband shows an unexampled capacity for growth and development, intellectual and spiritual, if not social, and the wife, remaining to the end the narrow rural aristocrat she was in the beginning, is decidedly left behind. The strange destiny which made the man who was to save the future of American democracy a typical American and a typical democrat was hardly equal to making him also an ideal husband, at any rate an ideal husband for such a wife. Mrs. Lincoln married Lincoln with condescension and hope that he might rise to her level, or even above it. He did, and so far as to be altogether beyond her limited power of ascent. She made a useful helpmate for a practical, aggressive lawyer in Springfield, Illinois. As the wife of the great, dreaming, smiling, creating democratic statesman of the modern world, she was just a trifle over-parted.

The difficulty of getting at the actual Mrs. Lincoln is extraordinary and exasperating. The cloud of anecdote and hearsay and gossip which envelops Lincoln himself, hangs even more impenetrably about her, because we have not the solid substance of her own words, as to a considerable extent we have his. There are but a few of her letters in print, and those few are not very significant. Many people have written about her, but they contradict one another, and misrepresent, according to their own prejudices and the strange passion for exalting Lincoln by either elevating or debasing everybody about him. How unsatisfactory the materials are

18

may be judged from the fact that the most illuminating document, on the whole, is the record of Mrs. Keckley, the colored seamstress at the White House. Mrs. Keckley was an intelligent observer, devoted to Mrs. Lincoln, and admitted to many intimate scenes and experiences. But I suppose few women would care to have their lives filtered to posterity through such a record. In short, I cannot ask my readers to give implicit belief to anything I say about Mrs. Lincoln, for I believe very little of it myself. Yet the difficulty of investigating her adds to the fascination. One sighs at times for such superb self-presentment as one gets in the letters of Sarah Butler or Harriet Blaine. But there is a peculiar pleasure in finding little hints and threads of suggestion and following them out patiently, even when they seem to lead nowhere.

The bare, indisputable facts in the life of Mary Todd Lincoln are few and simple. She was born of a good Kentucky family, in 1818, ten years after her husband. In 1839 she came to live with her sister, Mrs. Edwards, in Springfield. After a stormy courtship Lincoln married her in 1842. Her life then led her through Illinois law and politics to the White House, and the war, and the culmination of triumphant peace. All the triumph and hope were blasted by the assassination of her husband, and her remaining years, in spite of a brief sojourn in Europe, were darkened by sorrow and misfortune till a temperament, always impulsive and intense, was unbalanced to a point of oddity approaching and at times reaching actual derangement. She died in 1882.

In studying Mrs. Lincoln, one must admit that, while it is possible to get more or less reliable accounts of her external interests and activity, her inner life is almost hopelessly obscure. She had apparently a very good education, as educations went in Southern girls' schools in the middle of the nineteenth century. Mr. Rankin tells us that "while a resident of Springfield before and after her marriage, she impressed all who were acquainted with her with the excellent and accurate literary taste she had acquired by education and general reading, especially in history, poetry, and fiction." [1] But this was in a country town in 1840, and it must be remembered here, as elsewhere, that we are dealing with Mr. Rankin's kindly after-dinner memory. Education of a sort Mrs. Lincoln certainly had, education superior to that of many about her, and at any rate far superior to her husband's. She had also a nimble gift of words, and wrote with ease when she wished. Her natural intelligence was unquestionably shrewd, quick, and keen. Within her limits she saw into the nature of things and the motives of men, and she had a notable faculty of making observations upon them, often with a turn of wit and sarcasm which did not add to her popularity. That she had a trace of the larger humorous attitude seems unlikely, and it is still more unlikely that she ever grasped or enjoyed that attitude in the subtle, pervading, dissolving form in which it was constantly manifest in her husband. The element of Touchstone, of Charles Lamb, the instinct of remoteness, of detachment, even in the midst of vast tragic passions, perhaps most precisely in the midst of such, of illuminating them with the strange glory of laughter, which was so haunting and so fascinating in Lincoln, evidently annoyed and perplexed her, as it has many other excellent people.

If she read, we should like to know a little more definitely what she read. Mr. Rankin enlarges on her familiarity with French, as a matter of both reading and speaking, and assures us that she read the latest French literature.[2] I wonder if Sainte-Beuve was included in the list. I doubt it. Victor Hugo she did read, which perhaps is all one could expect.[3] She read current novels, since Lincoln writes to a friend in regard to one, "I am not much of a reader of this sort of literature; but my wife

21

got hold of the volume I took home, read it half through last night, and is greatly interested in it." [4] She liked to read aloud; [5] but what I should be glad to know is whether she was one of the two or three to whom Lincoln enjoyed reading aloud in quiet evenings; yet no one tells us. [6] And in the middle of an agitated night he used to traverse the White House corridors to read the trifles of Tom Hood to his sleepy secretaries; but I do not hear that he read them to her.

Again, we have little light as to other amusements of an intellectual order. There is no sign of any considerable æsthetic interest. Lincoln liked music, of a rather rudimentary type, but it does not appear that she played it to him. She does not seem to have cared for natural objects. Her husband enjoyed the pet goats who played about the White House. They bored her. [7] She liked to give away the flowers from the conservatory, but I do not read that she had a passion for them, any more than had Lincoln, who complained that he had "no taste natural or acquired for such things." [8] One pleasure they shared, that of the theater, and in Washington they were able to indulge this till it culminated in the performance that was ruinous for both.

As to Mrs. Lincoln's religion, there is a good deal to be said on the practical side. She was generous and kindly, ready to help and to give. Stoddard's account of her hospital visitation during the war is very attractive.[9] She made no display, sought no publicity whatever, but just went and gave and sympathized. In regard to the higher elements of spiritual life she was probably rather conventional, though she was a faithful member of the Episcopal, and then of the Presbyterian, Church, and Doctor Barton thinks that after her boy Willie's death she had some profounder religious experience. It may seem a trifling matter to note, but Mrs. Keckley's record of the ejaculation, "God, no!" as habitual seems to me singularly indicative of the woman.

I cannot think that there was much spiritual sympathy between her and her husband. We have, to be sure, Whitney's delightful sentence, "They were *en rapport* in all the higher objects of being." [10] I do not believe that anybody was really *"en rapport"* with Lincoln in such matters, and I certainly do not believe his wife was. They both had, indeed, a superstitious turn of mind, and when the husband had dreams of horror and foreboding, the wife was ready to accept and interpret them. But, in Mr. Stephenson's admirable phrase, Mrs. Lincoln's soul "inhabited the obvious." [11] The remote, gloomy spiritual regions haunted by him, whether he was smiling or praying, were hardly likely to be visited by her. Thousands of pages have been written about Lincoln's religion; but he still smiles and remains impenetrable. He practiced with God the same superb, shrewd opportunism by which, as contrasted with the dogmatic idealism of Jefferson Davis, he saved the American Union. With him, if ever with anyone, it seems a case for remembering Lamb's remark, which Lincoln would have thoroughly enjoyed, that he was determined his children should "be brought up in their father's religion—if they can find out what it is." [12] Yet it is curious that, after all, the practical, unmystical wife should have given us what is perhaps the very best summary on this point (italics mine): "Mr. Lincoln had no faith and no hope in the usual acceptation of those words. He never joined a church; but still, as I believe, he was a religious man by nature. . . . But it was *a kind of poetry in his nature,* and he was never a technical Christian." [13] Excellent example of the keen common sense of the woman who understands even where she is wholly unable to appreciate. And we come across this with Mrs. Lincoln at every turn.

II

In dealing with Mrs. Lincoln's external life we are on somewhat surer ground, though not much, for still the cloud of intangible gossip is likely to mislead us. Socially it is evident that she was ambitious and eager for success. On the whole, it cannot be said that she achieved it. Her appearance was by no means against her. Her face, in the photographs, is to me totally without charm. It is a positive, aggressive face, without a ray of sensitiveness in it. But, even in the heaviness of later years, she had a certain formal beauty and dignity, both of face and figure, and could bear herself well. It would seem that she dressed with taste, though at times too ostentatiously, and Lincoln objected to her extreme low necks.[14] As regards this matter of clothes I cannot resist quoting one passage, both because it is one of the few touches of real self-revelation that we have from her own pen and because it is so thoroughly human. Three years after her husband's death she writes to Mrs. Keckley: "I am positively dying with a broken heart, and the probability is that I shall be living but a *very* short time. May we all meet in a better world, where *such grief* is unknown. Write me all about yourself. I should like you to have about four black

25

widow's caps, just such as I had made in the fall in New York, sent to me. . . . The probability is that I shall need few more clothes; my rest, I am inclined to believe, *is near at hand.*" [15]

There are pleasant accounts of the Lincoln hospitality in Springfield. As to what happened in the White House observers differ. But it must be remembered that few hostesses have been subjected to such cruel criticism as Mrs. Lincoln had to meet. Those who watched her impartially, like W. H. Russell,[16] Bancroft,[17] and Laugel,[18] report in the main favorably, though it is noticeable that they are inclined to speak of her as better than they expected. The truth is, her ardent and impulsive temper made her tactless and uncertain. People could not count upon her, and it is said that she changed her intimates and social advisers too frequently.[19] The basis of her social zeal was rather an intense ambition than a broad human sympathy, and for the widest popularity and success the latter is indispensable. Then it must always be remembered that she had the strange, incalculable, most undomestic and unparlorable figure of Lincoln to carry with her, which would have been a terrible handicap to any woman. His dress was strange, his manners were strange, his talk was strange. And there was always that flood of homely stories,

26

reeking with the unexpected. He would not lay himself out to be agreeable to his wife's callers. Not that he was untidy. This is always justly denied. But he was magnificently inappropriate, disconcerting. One must not think of him as Dominie Sampson, but rather as if one were to attempt to introduce Charles Lamb or Shelley into a complicated conventional social life. So, if the poor lady failed, it must be admitted that she had her difficulties.

In her housekeeping and domestic arrangements she seems to have been excellent. Her table is highly spoken of and she was an exact and careful manager as to neatness and punctuality. Here again her husband was far from being a help to her. He was quite indifferent to what he ate and it was impossible to make him systematic about meals or hours generally. The remote world in which he lived was but imperfectly accessible to the tinkle of the dinner bell.

As regards the most essential element of domestic tranquillity, money, he was unsystematic also. In his legal business he could not be kept to exact accounting, had no commercial or speculative instinct whatever. Also, he was largely generous and more anxious to win his client's cause than to get his money. But he was no spender, had few needs and no costly tastes, and above all he abhorred debt, though circumstances sometimes forced him into it. How simple his financial ideas were appears in his reported remark shortly before his election as President: "I have a cottage at Springfield and about eight thousand dollars in money. . . . I hope I shall be able to increase it to twenty thousand, and that is as much as any man ought to want." [20] As a matter of fact, his estate was much larger than this at the time of his death.

Mrs. Lincoln no doubt did her best. In the early days she made her own dresses and she had always moments of violent economy. Her first remark to Mrs. Keckley was: "We are just from the West, and are poor. . . . If you will work cheap, you shall have plenty to do." [21] But her tastes in the matter of outlay were far different from her husband's. She liked to give, and did give. She liked the pleasant things of life, especially the kind that cost money. We have her own written words— and it is such a comfort when we do have them— on this subect: "When I saw the large steamers at the New York landing ready for the European voyage, I felt in my heart inclined to sigh that poverty was my portion. I often laugh and tell Mr. Lincoln that I am determined my next husband shall be rich." [22] Which of course was agreeable for him.

But the most pitiable exhibition in regard to Mrs. Lincoln's finances is Mrs. Keckley's story of the debts incurred from real or imagined necessities of dress to keep up the presidential dignity. The maddening pressure of these debts doubled the wife's anxiety as to the chances of her husband's second election in 1864. It must not be supposed that Mrs. Keckley's record of conversations that took place is verbally exact, but it is surely close to reality in its general tone. She says to Mrs. Lincoln, "And Mr. Lincoln does not even suspect how much you owe?" And the answer is, " 'God, no!' This was a favorite expression of hers. 'And I would not have him suspect. If he knew that his wife was involved to the extent that she is, the knowledge would drive him mad. He is so sincere and straightforward himself, that he is shocked by the duplicity of others. He does not know a thing about my debts, and I value his happiness, not to speak of my own, too much to allow him to know anything. This is what troubles me so much. If he is re-elected, I can keep him in ignorance of my affairs; but if he is defeated, then the bills will be sent in and he will know all.' " [23] Such are the domestic tragedies of money.

In her dealings with those about her in subordinate positions Mrs. Lincoln's uncertain temper is

said to have caused her a good deal of difficulty.
Herndon declares very definitely that "on account
of her peculiar nature she could not long retain
a servant in her employ." [24] But it is evident that
she was much attached to Mrs. Keckley, who served
her faithfully for a number of years. And the
testimony of the White House secretary, Stoddard,
is exceedingly friendly and favorable. She was considerate, he says, and did not burden you with
unreasonable demands. Probably, like many people
of quick temper, she regretted her outbursts and
did her best to make amends for them.

It is with her children that Mrs. Lincoln is most
attractive. Both she and Lincoln were devoted to
them, he in his gentle, humorous, abstracted fashion, she with no doubt erratic but effusive and genuine demonstrations of tenderness. She was interested in their education, in their health, in their
mental and moral development. But fate was as
cruel to her in the maternal as in the conjugal relation, and she lived to bury three of her four sons.
The eldest died in the early days in Springfield.
The youngest, Tad, who was her chief consolation
after her husband's death, so that she wrote, "Only
my darling Taddie prevents my taking my life," [25]
was snatched away in 1871. But the death of
Willie, in the midst of the at once anguished and

triumphant days in the White House, was the bitterest blow of all. The mother was inconsolable, and her grief led her into strange and fantastic ecstasies of passion, till the crisis came in the scene so vividly related by Mrs. Keckley, when Lincoln took his wife by the arm and led her to the window. "With a stately, solemn gesture, he pointed to the lunatic asylum, 'Mother, do you see that large white building on the hill yonder? Try to control your grief or it will drive you mad, and we may have to send you there.' " [26]

Yet, with the curious perversity of fortune which attended so much of Mrs. Lincoln's life, even her mother's sorrow, which would seem as if it ought to have won her public respect and doubtless did so, was turned by her inborn tactlessness into an element of unpopularity. The military band had been in the habit of playing in the square near the White House. But Mrs. Lincoln's reminiscent grief could not endure the music, and she insisted upon its being stopped for months, till the people became so indignant that Lincoln was forced to overrule her.[27] Truly, one cannot but sympathize with Mrs. Keckley's exclamation, even if it is a little exaggerated: "I never in my life saw a more peculiarly constituted woman. Search the world over, and you will not find her counterpart." [28] And she was married to a man as strange as herself, and as strangely different.

III

Now, having established Mrs. Lincoln's general character, as far as it is possible to do so, we come to the profoundly curious and interesting study of her relation with her husband, and this should begin with the history of their marriage.

In early life Lincoln seems to have had a susceptible imagination with regard to women, the more susceptible, perhaps, because he had so little to do with them. His profound affection in his twenties for Ann Rutledge, which has been embroidered by so many story-tellers, and her melancholy death, almost unhinged him for the time, and Herndon insists that he never really loved anyone afterward. But a varied list of feminine names appears. There is the robust Mary Owens, with whom his courtship seems mainly to have consisted in endeavors to persuade her that she would do better not to marry him. There is a more shadowy Sarah Rickard. And there is Matilda Edwards, sister-in-law of the lady with whom her own sister, Mary Todd, was also staying. But the substantial charms of Mary and her decided habit of getting what she wanted, in the end fixed the rather wandering·lover, and in 1840 they were definitely engaged.

Here we strike one of the most debated points in Mrs. Lincoln's life, and in dealing with the course of this engagement we are at once confronted with the question of the veracity of Herndon. It seems to me that his essential tone and attitude must be regarded as satisfactory. He ventured a prophetic protest against the drift of a silly legendary atmosphere tending to envelop Lincoln as it enveloped Washington. Such a tendency evinces much more the timidity of the worshiper than the greatness of the idol, for if he is really great, nothing will make him more so than to prove that he was really human. At the same time, after the industrious researches of Miss Tarbell, it is difficult to accept in detail Herndon's account of the stormy progress of Lincoln's love-affair. According to Herndon, the day for the wedding was actually fixed, the supper was ordered, the bride arrayed, the parson present— and the bridegroom failed to appear, tormented by doubts and hesitations approaching mental derangement. The disturbance was so great that Lincoln's friends for a time feared suicide.

Without pronouncing positively on the more highly colored details of this narrative, we may regard the indisputable facts as curious enough.

It is certain that the engagement was broken, certain that Lincoln a year later referred to the "fatal first of January, 1841," the day which, according to Herndon, was set for the wedding. Also, we have the remarkable series of letters to Speed, a near friend who was wooing and marrying at the same time, in which Lincoln uncovers his tormented soul, a soul clearly well versed in all the tortures of self-analysis, self-criticism, and self-reproach. Long before this crisis he had written to Mary Owens: "Whatever woman may cast her lot with mine, should anyone ever do so, it is my intention to do all in my power to make her happy and contented, and there is nothing I can imagine that would make me more unhappy than to fail in the effort." [29] In March, 1842, he writes to Speed that, since the breaking of his engagement he "should have been entirely happy but for the never-absent idea that there is one still unhappy whom I have contributed to make so. That kills my soul. I cannot but reproach myself for even wishing to be happy while she is otherwise." [30]

Then Speed is married and likes it, which impresses Lincoln, and somehow or other Mary regains her control, and on the 4th of November, 1842, the two are married very simply and quietly. In a letter of Lincoln's only recently published there is this admirable phrase, turned with a delicate significance which Lamb or Touchstone might have envied, "Nothing new here, except my marrying, which to me is a matter of profound wonder." [31]

It is matter of profound wonder to most of us, and we endeavor, without much success, to find out how it happened. To begin with, what was Mary's motive, why did a woman so proud as she seek to retain a lover who appeared so obviously reluctant? Herndon's theory is fantastic. He asserts that Mary's pride was so bitterly wounded that she married Lincoln to make his life miserable, purely for revenge. Even put in more rational fashion, with the idea that she was a person who persisted relentlessly in getting what she had once wanted, the explanation is scanty. There is also the theory that Mary was ambitious and that she foresaw Lincoln's future, even preferring him in this regard to so promising a candidate as Douglas. Something there may be in this: she was a keen-sighted woman, and she is said to have prognosticated her husband's success from the start. But I think we must add that she loved him, felt instinctively the charm that so many men felt, the almost inexplicable charm which went with that strange, ungainly physical make-up of which an early friend could say, "he was the *ungodliest* figure I ever saw." [32]

In the same way I feel that probably something in her fascinated Lincoln. His conscience forced him, say some; her family forced him, say others. Both may have contributed. He was morbidly sensitive. He was indolent and in some ways easily led. Yet I have no doubt he loved her, and that quick, narrow, masterful spirit gained and kept a hold over his vaguer and more fluid one.

I imagine that the love on both sides persisted to the end. Herndon insists that there was no love at all. To Mr. Rankin the whole affair apparently seems a sweet idyl of uninterrupted bliss. It was probably just an average earthly marriage, with an increasing bond of association overcoming all sorts of wear and tear and pulling and hauling. Lincoln could never have been a comfortable husband for any wife. His casual ways, his irregular habits, his utter disregard of the conventions and small proprieties would have worn on a far more tranquil temper than Mary Todd's. And her temper was not tranquil at all; in fact, patience was the least of her distinguishing qualities. Her violent outbursts on small occasions are matter of record, and it is impossible to put aside altogether the scenes of furious, disgraceful public jealousy described by Badeau [33] and confirmed by General Sherman. [34] Lincoln took it all quietly, though it must have wrung his heart, patted her on the shoulder, called her his child-wife, and she was ashamed of herself—and did it again.

It was an every-day marriage, with some rather dark spots in it, but hardly so bad as has been represented. They loved their children and called each other "father" and "mother," in the old homely way, and their hearts grew more and more bound up in each other, and they just took life as it came. There is the cruel saying of La Rochefoucauld, "there are comfortable marriages, but no delicious ones," which simply means that life, as we go on with it, with all its trials, may at its best be comfortable, but can rarely be delicious. There is the other saying of the French comic writer, "in marriage, when love exists, familiarity kills it; when it does not exist, it gives it birth." Both have a certain significance in connection with the marriage of the Lincolns.

But what has afforded infinite entertainment to the inquiring biographer, and what I think must be equally entertaining to the judicious reader, is the violent contrast with which the same simple facts may be stated according to the prejudice of the person who states them. Take the two extremes, Herndon and Mr. Rankin: their analysis of Lincoln's married life cannot but be instructive as well as diverting.

First, there is Lincoln's absence from home. He left on every excuse, Herndon says. He lived in his office. Where other lawyers returned from their work to the comfortable fireside, he lingered in the country store or anywhere, rather than face the nagging that daily tormented him. All a mistake, says Mr. Rankin. He was a great deal from home, attending to more or less important business, and why? Because he had such a competent, careful, devoted wife that his presence at home was entirely unnecessary.

Take clothing. Mrs. Lincoln was always fussing about her husband's dress. Again, explains the unfailing Mr. Rankin, this was all a matter of health. He was threatened with consumption and her loving care in seeing that he was properly clothed may have saved his life. It was the same with food and regularity at meals. Innumerable stories are told of her sending arbitrarily at the most inconvenient times to insist upon his attendance, and even appearing herself, with some indulgence of shrewish tongue. Wrong, wrong, urges Mr. Rankin. She may have spoken quickly, but affectionate anxiety about his health was at the bottom of it all.

The best is the story of the ring. Herndon enlarges, with rather fiendish satisfaction, upon Lincoln's reluctance when even the *bona fide* wedding day arrived. Speed's little boy, says Herndon, seeing the bridegroom so finely dressed, inquired where he was going. "To hell, I suppose," was the gloomy answer.[35] Oh, cries Mr. Rankin, cruel, cruel, even to imagine that he could have uttered such a word! There was the wedding ring. Did not Lincoln have engraved in it the tender sentiment, "Love is eternal"?[36] Innocent Mr. Rankin! he apparently does not remember Jaques's remark to Orlando: "You are full of pretty answers. Have you not been acquainted with goldsmiths' wives and conned them out of rings?" I will not suggest that the sentiment may have emanated from Mary herself, though there have been such instances. But, alas! we know how many rings with similar mottoes are clasping unloved and loveless fingers all about the world. And always, to sum the whole, there is the cynical, cruel, profound, significant sentence of Dumas *fils: "Dans le mariage, quand l'amour existe, l'habitude le tue; quand il n'existe pas, il le fait naître."*

IV

Having thus analyzed, with delightful inconclusiveness, the conjugal affection of the Lincolns, we may consider with equal inconclusiveness, the important question of Mrs. Lincoln's influence over her husband. It is clear that she was a person who naturally tended to dominate those about her. Could she dominate him? In little things he was no doubt yielding enough, to her and to others, as appears from his jocose remark that it was fortunate he was not a woman, since he never could say no. When it came to great matters, especially moral, he may not have bothered to say no, but he did what he thought right, without the slightest regard to the demands of others. Hear what Mrs. Lincoln says herself: "Mr. Lincoln was mild in his manners, but he was a terribly firm man when he set his foot down. None of us, no man or woman, could rule him after he had once fully made up his mind." [37] Can you not read the outcome of many fruitless battles here? Mrs. Edwards gives a pretty picture of the wooer's absorbed attention during their courtship, how Mary talked and Lincoln listened.[38] No doubt he listened all his life. Sometimes he heeded.

Mrs. Lincoln's chief wrestle was with her husband's social peculiarities. Here she was obviously in part successful and it cannot be questioned that her experience and knowledge of the world were of great benefit. As Newton puts it, she "taught him particularly that there was such a thing as society, which observed a man's boots as well as his principles." [39] At the same time, from his boots to his hat, and through all the long six feet between, the man was thoroughly unconventional and nothing could make him otherwise. In the early married days in Springfield he would open the door himself in his shirt sleeves and assure august visitors that his wife would be down as soon as she could get her trotting harness on.[40] Such things torment any well-constituted woman. Mary resented them. Yet she was sweetly contrite afterward. When a friend said to her, "Mary, if I had a husband with such a mind as yours has, I wouldn't care what he did," she answered, "It is foolish—it is a small thing to complain of." [41] The oddities may have been toned down a little in Washington; but they were never got rid of. You could believe in the man, you could admire him, you could scold him; but you could not domesticate him.

On broader matters, less naturally within her sphere, even on the conduct of the war, Mrs. Lincoln evidently had her word. What wife would not? And sometimes it was the apt and poignant one. How characteristic is her retort to Stanton, who proposed to have her painted as she appeared at Fort Stevens, when she had come under fire:

41

"That is very well, and I can assure you of one thing, Mr. Secretary, if I had had a few *ladies* with me, the rebels would not have been permitted to get away as they did." [42] Large military policy was perhaps beyond her, but she gave her sharp, quick judgment of military commanders, bearing out, to some extent, her husband's admission that she had quicker insight into character than he.[43] The words, as reported by Mrs. Keckley, can hardly be relied upon; but the general drift of them must be accurate. Of McClellan she said: "He is a humbug. . . . He talks so much and does so little. If I had the power, I would very soon take off his head and put some energetic man in his place." [44] As to Grant, she is equally severe: "He is a butcher and is not fit to be the head of an army. . . . He has no management, no regard for life. . . . I could fight an army as well myself." [45] How perfect is Lincoln's quiet answer to all this: "Well, mother, supposing that we give you command of the army. No doubt you would do much better than any general that has been tried." [46]

With politics Mrs. Lincoln was of course more interested and more at home than in military details. She watched her husband's career from the time of her earliest acquaintance with him and followed every step of it with the intensest ardor. Lincoln's appreciation of this shows most charmingly in his remark, on first hearing the result of the presidential nomination in 1860, that there was "a little short woman at our house who is probably more interested in this dispatch than I am; and if you will excuse me, gentlemen, I will take it up and let her see it." * [47] Abstract political principles may not have appealed to her much. Before the war her sympathies were more or less Southern, and this brought her criticism and added to the unpopularity which she was not able to overcome. But there can be no question about her entire loyalty to her husband's cause, which was in every sense her own. And whenever there was a personal point to be decided, her judgment was always quick and sometimes sure. It is only just to say that I have not found one single case of her attempting to exert influence for the benefit of her friends or family, no soliciting of offices or commissions where they were not deserved. But she did interfere when her husband's, and her own, interests seemed to be involved. It was she who prevented

---

* It is profitable to compare this remark, as thus reported by Lamon, with the refined, genteel version given by Mr. Rankin (*Personal Recollections of Abraham Lincoln,* page 190), "There is a lady, over yonder on Eighth Street, who is deeply interested in this news; I will carry it to her." Very likely neither version represents what Lincoln actually said; but the Rankin method is always the same.

Lincoln from accepting the governorship of Oregon in 1849, from political foresight, say Lamon and Mr. Rankin, because she did not want to go off into the woods, say Nicolay and Hay. And in other cases she exerted a pressure which was strong and perhaps effective.

As in army matters, so in politics, it was the human side which interested her, and she criticized Seward and Chase just as savagely as she criticized Grant.[48] Also, she was much inclined to work on human agents where it was possible. Russell complains that she was accessible to flattery and filled her parlors with "men who would not be received in any respectable private house in New York." [49] Her own explanation of this proceeding, in the dialogue with Mrs. Keckley, bearing on the election of 1864, is profoundly interesting: "In a political canvass it is policy to cultivate every element of strength. These men have influence, and we require influence to re-elect Mr. Lincoln. I will be clever to them until after the election, and then, if we remain at the White House, I will drop every one of them, and let them know very plainly that I only made tools of them. They are an unprincipled set, and I don't mind a little double-dealing with them." When Mrs. Keckley inquires if Mr. Lincoln knows, the answer is: "God, no! he would never sanction such a proceeding, so I keep him in the dark and will not tell him till all is over." [50] Somehow in all these political concerns Mrs. Lincoln reminds one at times of Mr. Strachey's Victoria. There is the same dignified, yet dumpy figure, the same round, hard, positive, dominating face. And one cannot but think of the remark of an Englishman to Mrs. Fields, which Mr. Strachey would enjoy. "We call her 'Her *Un*gracious Majesty.' " [51]

It is clear enough that back of Mrs. Lincoln's political interest and indeed back of all her life there was a tremendous driving force of ambition. There is much debate whether she had more ambition or he. They were different in this, as in everything. His ambition was vague, dreamy, fitful, mystical. Hers was narrower, more concrete, but it never rested, and went straight at its ends. How much we are to believe of the apparently well-authenticated stories of her aiming at the White House almost from girlhood, is a question. Any girl may aim at the White House, I suppose. No doubt a good many do who never get there. Perhaps the most impressive anecdote on the subject is Lamon's account of his first talk with her, in 1847. "Yes," she said, of her husband, "he is a great favorite everywhere. He is to be President of the United States some day; if I had not thought so, I never would have married him, for you can see he is not pretty. But look at him! Doesn't he look as if he would make a magnificent President?" [52] That a woman should speak thus in her first interview with a stranger is extraordinarily suggestive, if you can believe it. And Lamon's emphatic insistence upon her use of the word "magnificent" makes the story somewhat more credible.

At any rate, she got to the White House and reigned there through four of the greatest years in the history of the country. I wish I had a little more authority for the seemingly sane and not unfavorable account of her White House career given by Mr. Willis Steell, [53] the immense effort for popularity and social success and supremacy, ending in satiety and disappointment: "The 'court' she set up had turned into a mock bubble, shining in iridescent colors only in her imagination; created from sordid materials, and wholly empty." [54] Then the triumphant election of 1864 set the crown upon it all, if crown there was. In April, 1865, the war was over. On the afternoon of the 14th Mr. and Mrs. Lincoln drove out alone together and Lincoln seemed singularly happy, so much so that Mary's ill-divining soul presaged the woe to come. He

46

talked to her of well-earned rest, of peaceful plans and projects for the future. In the evening they went to Ford's Theater. And still his mind was rather on the coming dreamy years than on the play. We will go to Europe, he said to her, go to the Holy Land, go to the city I have always wanted to see, Jerusalem—[55] While he was busy with such thought, the pistol of Wilkes Booth shattered the world of Mary Todd Lincoln into diminutive fragments, which no man ever again could piece together.

v

As this portrait is mainly made up of questions that cannot be answered, we might as well conclude with the most unanswerable of all: would Lincoln's career have been different, for better or worse, if he had married a different wife? Here again a variety of speculations present themselves, each urged with partisan eagerness. It would perhaps be possible to work out some such theory as Mr. Van Wyck Brooks cleverly applied to the case of Mark Twain—that is, that the constant conventionalizing pressure of a prosaic wife chilled and deadened, to some extent, the quick burst of spontaneous genius; but we should always have to re-

member that Mark was passionately devoted to
Livy from beginning to end. There is, on the
whole, a singular unanimity of biographers, in
the view that Mrs. Lincoln was helpful to her husband; but there is an astonishing difference as to
the way she helped. Herndon, always critical, admits the helpfulness, in fact emphasizes it. Lincoln,
he says, was naturally indolent, contented, stay-at-
home (though elsewhere he calls him ambitious).
If home had been delightful, he would have enjoyed
it and would not have been so eager to make a mark
in the world. Mary made home hideous, and by so
doing made her husband great. Mr. Rankin does
his best to involve this cynical explanation in the
rosy mist of his amiable memory, and goes to the
other extreme. According to him Mary was a sort
of protecting angel, who advised, cautioned, impelled, always at the right time. "Without Mary
Todd for his wife, Abraham Lincoln would never
have been President. Without Abraham Lincoln
for her husband, Mary Todd would, probably, never
have been a President's wife." [56] This beatific solution may be correct; but if it is so, I find it difficult to explain the fact that, though Nicolay and
Hay were intimately present in the White House,
in all the ten volumes of their *History* Mrs. Lincoln
gets only a few lines here and there, and in the

close daily record of Hay's *Diary* her name is hardly mentioned. Surely a guardian, ministering angel would deserve and receive a little more than this. For myself, I find Mr. Stephenson's moderate statement very satisfying: "She had certain qualities that her husband lacked. . . . She had that intuition for the main chance which shallow people confound with practical judgment. Her soul inhabited the obvious." [57] Lincoln's natural danger was the world of dreams and going astray in it, says Mr. Stephenson: "That this never occurred may be fairly credited, or at least very plausibly credited, to the firm-willed, the utterly matter-of-fact little person he had married." [58]

The problem of Lincoln's melancholy brings the question of his life with Mary to a point, that haunting, brooding sadness, which rarely left him, though he shot the dark cloud through with constant fantastic sallies of laughter, that sadness which Herndon expressed with such extraordinary power when he said that "melancholy dripped from him as he walked," [59] and which Lincoln himself described as so terrible that "if what I feel were equally distributed to the whole human family, there would not be one cheerful face on the earth." [60] Did Mary cause this grief or did she alleviate it? Herndon by no means affirms the former, but he evidently thinks that the misery of home surroundings much augmented a constitutional tendency.[61] Then along comes Mr. Rankin, from whom a mellow optimism is constantly dripping, and assures us that, on the contrary, so far from causing the melancholy, Mary was the one who could cure it. When the spells grew acute, "she . . . was the only one who had the skill and tact to shorten their duration. . . . I revere her memory for this most gracious service." [62] Again Mr. Rankin may be correct; but when I think of that concise, hard, unsympathetic face, I wonder.

Among the varied possibilities connected with Lincoln's other early loves, the suggestion of melancholy brings up most of all the image of Ann Rutledge. It has even been suggested that the melancholy had its origin in the loss of her of whom he said, the thought of "the snows and rains falling upon her grave filled him with indescribable grief." [63] If he had married Ann, would it all have been different? We know so little of her that we cannot conjecture further than that a devoted, self-forgetful passion such as he hardly felt for Mary Todd might have changed his world. As for the substantial, hearty Mary Owens, it is not likely that his experience with her would have been very different from his experience with the other Mary.

And then one thinks of a woman of real genius, of large capacity, of sweet human comprehension, a woman like Theodosia Burr or Sarah Butler. With a wife like this would Lincoln have done, perhaps not greater things, but done them with an ampler serenity and spiritual peace?

I doubt it. Lincoln was not in any way a woman's man, in spite of the early loves. Mary Owens thought him "deficient in those little links which make up the chain of woman's happiness." [64] Lincoln himself, much later, wrote, in his dry way, "The truth is, I have never corresponded much with ladies; and hence I postpone writing letters to them, as a business I do not understand." [65] He may have been a master of men; for dealing with women he was at once too self-contained and too sincere. I am sure the words of the *Imitation* would have pleased him: "Be not a friend to any one woman in particular, but commend all good women in general to God."

More than that, he lived in a solitude which neither man nor woman ever perfectly penetrated. No doubt we all live in such a solitude. The difference is that nine hundred and ninety-nine out of a thousand rarely think of it. Lincoln thought of it all the time. He ruled over millions of men and women who loved him; yet he was enormously

51

alone, because he felt himself to be so. In this one point there is a curious resemblance between him and the greatest of all his contemporaries, a man who differed from him in so many other respects, Robert E. Lee. Lee was lonely as Lincoln was. Yet Lee had a most exquisite, devoted, sympathizing wife and children whose affection was constant and complete. The loneliness, with him, as with Lincoln, was that isolation of the human soul which the yearning of the deepest love merely accentuates. Lincoln's own words to Speed convey it with clarifying intensity, "I have no doubt it is the peculiar misfortune of both you and me to dream dreams of Elysium far exceeding all that anything earthly can realize." [66] When there was such an ideal as this to compete with, neither the perfection of wit, nor of beauty, nor of sacrifice, would have been any more satisfying than poor Mary Todd.

III

MRS. BENEDICT ARNOLD

CHRONOLOGY

Margaret Shippen Arnold.

Born, Philadelphia, June 11, 1760.

Married Benedict Arnold, April 8, 1779.

Arnold fled from West Point to the British, September 25, 1780.

Joined husband in New York, November, 1780.

Went to England, December, 1781.

Husband died, June 14, 1801.

Died, London, August 24, 1804.

MRS. BENEDICT ARNOLD

I

In one of the fragments of the old Greek dramatists a tragic heroine pathetically describes the contrast in the life of a woman tenderly brought up in her father's house, shielded, petted, protected from all shocks and storms, then suddenly thrust out, perhaps when little more than a girl, into the great tumult of the world, yoked to a man of whom she may know nothing fundamentally, and forced to take her full part in all the struggles and battles and miseries of life. It was an old story in Sophocles's day. It is an older story now. But it is a true story always, and rarely has it been illustrated with more pathos and passion than in the case of Margaret Shippen Arnold. She was gently, affectionately nurtured, if ever girl was. Then at nineteen she attached herself to the fortunes of Benedict Arnold, and was buffeted about the world in a fashion far different from what her youth might have led her to expect.

The Shippens were a prominent family in Philadelphia before the Revolution, active in public affairs and much respected. Margaret's father, Edward, was educated to the law in England and was always supposed to be, like others of his class, reluctant to see a separation from the mother country. At the same time, he was certainly not a decided Tory, resented the encroachments of George the Third's government, and retained the respect of all his fellow citizens so much that, after independence was established, he was made Chief Justice of Pennsylvania, and performed his duties with usefulness and dignity. Margaret was born in 1760 and had several brothers and sisters. Her father's comment on her birth was, "My Peggy this morning made me a present of a fine baby, who though of the worst sex, is yet entirely welcome." [1] Devotion to her father seems to have been a marked characteristic, and we are told that in her childhood she made "his comfort her leading thought, often preferring to remain with him when evening parties and amusements would attract her sisters from home." [2] Of her mother's influence or importance in her life we get no mention, and the little notice taken of her in letters of later years would not indicate that the maternal impression was very strong. The girl was undoubtedly well educated in all social accomplishments and graces, and the practical side was not neglected, as appears in her successful business management at a later period, which she attributes to her father, who gave her "the most useful and best education that America at that time afforded." [3] But there is no evidence of any intellectual training or interest. Nor does her tone at any time suggest marked religious surroundings.

In spite of Margaret's taste for the domestic hearth, it is evident that the Shippens were social in their habits, and she was swept into the whirl like the rest. Her father complains, like other fathers, of the expense of carrying on his household: "Tne style of life my fashionable daughters have introduced into my family, and their dress, will, I fear, before long oblige me to change the scene." [4] Both her portraits and tradition show that Margaret was very lovely, blond, with a face that must have been gay and tender and responsive, not by any means intellectual, but quick and keen and capable of mischief. Washington declared at a somewhat later period that all the young men were in love with Mrs. Arnold,[5] and the disease seems to have been catching at all times. When the British occupied Philadelphia in 1778, there was an abundance of social gayety. In the wild farrago of diversions, called the Mischianza, the Shippen girls were to have taken a prominent part, but this was thwarted by their father's reluctance to have them appear in public in Turkish costumes. Major André, who was one of the chief organizers of this festivity, was on friendly terms with the family and at one time painted a charming portrait of Margaret, to whom he afterward wrote a letter from New York, with courteous offers of service, a letter perfectly innocent in aspect, and probably in intent, but in view of final events considerably suggestive of disaster.

Then the British evacuated the city, the Americans took possession of it, and Benedict Arnold was made military governor. Arnold was nearly twenty years older than Margaret. He was a widower with children. He was disabled by a wounded leg. But his quick, emotional nature enjoyed the luxury of his Philadelphia surroundings, enjoyed the contrast between the rough discipline of camps and the merry atmosphere of jest and gayety. Also, he was distinctly susceptible to feminine charm. Only six months earlier he had wooed —unsuccessfully—a certain Miss DeBlois of Boston, writing her these ardent, if somewhat stilted phrases: "Friendship and esteem founded on the merit of the object is the most certain basis to build a lasting happiness upon, and when there is a tender

MRS. BENEDICT ARNOLD

and ardent passion on one side, and friendship and esteem on the other, the heart must be callous to every tender sentiment if the taper of love is not lighted up at the flame." [6]

Then Arnold came across Miss Shippen, was at once enchanted, and the flame which had burned so brightly for Miss DeBlois was soon transferred to the newer object. After a very brief delay, he proposed himself to Edward Shippen as a son-in-law, disclaiming all considerations of fortune, and expressing the hope that "our difference in political sentiments will be no bar to my happiness." [7] At the same time he urged his suit with the daughter, wrote a long letter containing the warmest expressions of devotion, and embodied in it various portions of the letter written six months before to Miss DeBlois, notably the above sentence, practically word for word. I strive in vain to picture to myself the lover's state of mind when he did this. Was there just the hint of a cynical smile about the mouth of the man of thirty-eight, who thought he had learned what women liked to have said to them? Or did the rough, eager soldier really imagine that, having once hit upon the finest possible utterance of romantic affection, it would be vain to try to improve it?

And how did it all strike Margaret? That is

what we shall never exactly know. There seems to be little doubt that her father was opposed to the match, as well he might be. Arnold was only a soldier of fortune, and the girl was a mere child. But fathers, no matter how much one has cherished them, count for little in such cases. Apparently there was some hesitation. A cousin writes: "Pray tell me, will cousin Peggy follow your example. . . . Does she know her own mind yet?" [8] And another: "A lame leg is at present the only obstacle. But a lady who makes that the only objection, and is firmly persuaded it will soon be well, can never retract, however expressly conditional an engagement may have been made." [9] Should not you like to have heard Arnold's wooing? Do you suppose it was in the style of the letter to Miss DeBlois, or something altogether different? Mrs. Arnold's engaging biographer and relative, who has an almost superhuman gift for deducing something from nothing, proves Margaret's extreme modesty by the following sentence of a letter to Franklin from his daughter concerning his infant granddaughter: "You can't think how fond of kissing she is, and she gives such old-fashioned smacks General Arnold says he would give a good deal to have her for a schoolmistress to teach the young ladies how to kiss." [10] From which we are invited to infer that Miss Shippen was not an adept at kissing. Oh, really — !

At any rate, kissing or no kissing, Margaret made up her mind to marry her middle-aged hero. As Weir Mitchell puts it in regard to this case: "When a delicate-minded, sensitive, well-bred woman falls in love with a strong, coarse, passionate man, there is no more to be said except 'take her.'" [11] And, having made up her mind, she did not allow a wounded leg to stand in the way. An eye-witness describes the wedding, which took place on the 8th of April, 1779: "Arnold during the marriage ceremony was supported by a soldier, and when seated his disabled limb was propped upon a camp-stool." [12] So, like the tragic heroine of Sophocles, this daintily nurtured girl took the arm of an adventurous warrior and stepped out into the wide, uncertain world.

II

And it was an uncertain world. Arnold's plans and status were far from fixed. He had not been promoted as he hoped, and his wound made a military career more difficult. At one time before his marriage he even thought of retiring upon a farm and announced that his ambition was to be

"a good citizen rather than shining in history." [13]
I hardly imagine that a farm would have suited
Margaret. Instead, they settled down in Philadelphia and led a gay and expensive life. Arnold
bought the beautiful and costly estate of Mount
Pleasant and they entertained freely. Arnold liked
the display and the distinction, and his wife liked
the fun. If they spent largely, the fault was mainly
his. She was a child and spent what he gave her and
did what he told her, no doubt, and their tastes
agreed admirably in wanting a good time in the
world.

But the money had to be found somehow. Arnold
got involved in hazy speculation, sure to be disastrous for a military commander. He was by no
means popular with the Philadelphia citizens or
with Congress, and he was shortly accused of dubious transactions amounting to peculation, and
tried by court-martial. He defended himself with
energy and on the whole with success, and was
practically acquitted; but the court concluded that
his conduct had been indiscreet enough to require
a reprimand from Washington, which was duly,
though gently, administered. It is easy to conceive
how Arnold's pride was stung and how keenly his
wife must have felt the affront and what she considered persecution.

The trial was completed in January, 1780. During the spring Arnold's movements were uncertain and he was haunted by various vague projects. In March a son was born. When summer came, Arnold succeeded in getting Washington to give him the command of West Point, and after more or less prolonged correspondence with the British he agreed to surrender the fortress. In September Mrs. Arnold, with her infant, joined her husband. The negotiations came to a crisis toward the end of the month. André had his interview with Arnold and was captured on his return with incriminating papers. Washington arrived at West Point the following morning, but not quite soon enough to intercept Arnold, who received word of what had happened and made a hurried escape. He was sitting at breakfast when the message was brought. He excused himself, and his wife followed him. In her room he broke the news to her, left her almost distracted, flung himself on the first horse he could get, and fled down the river to the British. When Mrs. Arnold had recovered from her insanity of grief and bewilderment, Washington offered to send her either to her husband in New York or to her father in Philadelphia. She accepted the latter arrangement.

Such is the succinct, external account of the great

tragedy of Margaret Arnold's life. But just here
arises one of those puzzles which are the torment,
and the charm, of the biographer's business, one
of those problems which can never be quite settled,
because the data are insufficient, yet must be dealt
with and disposed of with some sort of a conclusion,
as definite as possible.

In 1836, fifty-six years after Arnold's treason,
Matthew L. Davis published the "Memoirs of
Aaron Burr," relying mainly upon information
furnished by Burr himself. In the first volume of
this work Davis relates that Mrs. Arnold, on her
return from West Point to Philadelphia, stopped
at the house of Mrs. Prevost at Paramus. There
was some acquaintance between the ladies, Mrs.
Arnold having already stayed there on her former
trip, and as Mrs. Prevost was entirely British in
sympathy, so soon as Mrs. Arnold arrived she threw
off the mask, declared that she was weary of acting,
that she had been all along cognizant of what was
going on and had even urged and persuaded her
husband to the step he had taken. Mrs. Prevost,
who was herself, by the way, one of the noblest
and most charming of women, was afterward married to Burr, and, according to Davis, told her husband this story.[14]

Burr's later biographer, Parton, repeats the

narrative with considerable variants, but without giving any authority for these whatever. According to him Burr was actually present at the scene between Mrs. Arnold and Mrs. Prevost, and whatever report he made of it was that of an eye and ear witness.[15] Davis further supports his story by an account of a visit made by Mrs. Arnold early in the summer to her friends the Morrises, during which she was informed that her husband had received another appointment instead of West Point, information which was said to have thrown her into a state of extreme distress.[16] But evidently this might have been explicable in other ways.

Supposing we were to accept the story of Burr as it comes through Davis and Parton, what would it mean? Here was a girl of twenty, placed in one of the most tremendous tragic crises that could come upon a human being, exposed to the criticism of the keenest and most watchful eyes, and sustaining herself by acting, which, if it was acting, must have been superb. We have abundance of record from witnesses of her bearing immediately after Arnold's departure. Perhaps the account of Alexander Hamilton, who, as a young soldier under Washington, was present and wrote to his betrothed, Miss Schuyler, is the most vivid: "She, for a time, entirely lost herself. The general went up to see her, and she upbraided him with being in a plot to murder her child. One moment she raved, another she melted into tears. . . . All the sweetness of beauty, all the loveliness of innocence, all the tenderness of a wife, and all the fondness of a mother showed themselves in her appearance and conduct. We have every reason to believe that she was entirely unacquainted with the plan, and that the first knowledge of it was when Arnold went to tell her he must banish himself from his country and from her forever. She instantly fell into a convulsion, and he left her in that situation." [17] Surely neither Mrs. Siddons nor Rachel could have done better. The same testimony comes from Varicks and Franks, Arnold's aides, who had even ampler opportunities of observation. Varicks said, when on oath, "Not long after you mentioned your suspicions to me Mrs. Arnold called for me, and when I waited on her I found from her language and conduct that she was in great distress and had lost her reason, but could not divine the cause. . . . Mrs. Arnold recovering her reason in some measure complained to me that she was left without a friend." [18]

In view of this evidence and much more of the same nature, historians generally refuse to believe Mrs. Arnold guilty in any way. If that is the case, what becomes of Burr's story? The explanation of Mrs. Arnold's ardent and affectionate biographers is perfectly simple: Burr lied. This explanation is carried much further into an elaborate development as to why and how he lied. It seems that a tradition survives in the Shippen family to the effect that Burr, who had long been intimate with Mrs. Arnold's relatives, offered to conduct her from Mrs. Prevost's to Philadelphia, and that on the way he made love to her and was indignantly repelled. In consequence he invented the slander to get his revenge.[19] On the basis of this vague legend and a much vaguer paragraph in a letter, mildly referring to a young gentleman, not named, whose "conduct was not quite agreeable to our notions of propriety," [20] and whose apologies may have been acceptable to Mrs. Arnold and may not, the biographer weaves the most extraordinary circumstantial narrative of Burr's attempted seduction of the distressed lady, a narrative cunningly devised to impose on the simple as fact, but with no solid foundation of evidence.[21] And observe the delightful possibilities of argument in such subtle and complicated matters. Burr's partial biographer insists that his hero carefully refrained from telling the story until no one was left alive who could be harmed by the telling of it as a matter of historical

record. Mrs. Arnold's biographer is equally insistent that Burr's object was not to promulgate his
slander until there was no one who could contradict
him. So our motives are bandied and tossed about
by those who are chiefly anxious to use them for
their own purposes.

All this fantastic myth about Burr's malignity I
instantly and totally reject, on *a priori* grounds. I
have studied him long and intimately and in many
respects I regard him with affection, in some with
admiration, though hardly with esteem. His general attitude and conduct toward women was reprehensible beyond belief, and I think it not out of
the question that he may have seized what seemed to
him a favorable opportunity to make love to Mrs.
Arnold, or to appear to do so. But, no matter
how this wooing was received, it is preposterous
to suppose that he should have gone out of his way
to invent such a circumstantial story and then deliberately circulate it fifty years afterward. With all
Burr's faults, I believe that when he said he had
"no memory for injuries," [22] he was mainly correct.
If I were forced to choose between the two alterna-
tives, Mrs. Arnold's acting or Burr's deliberate
slander, I should not hesitate a moment.

But I do not think we need be reduced to this.
Independent of Burr, there is no evidence against

the lady that counts, since the one letter written to her by André and already referred to cannot be treated as such. And as regards Burr's story, there is clearly the largest room for possible misunderstandings. Parton's and Davis's versions vary greatly, they both must have come through a considerable number of sources, and both are late in date; therefore it is easy to suppose that Mrs. Prevost misunderstood Mrs. Arnold, and Burr Mrs. Prevost, and Davis Burr, and Parton everybody, as he was too liable to do. As I have said, the great majority of historians exculpate Mrs. Arnold altogether, and on the whole I am not inclined to differ from them.

To be sure, she was very lovely. Washington's remark that all the young men were in love with her is not to be forgotten, and old historians are quite as susceptible as young soldiers. There is always Rosalind's cynical warning in regard to Nature's dealings with the fair sex, "Those that she makes fair she scarce makes honest, and those that she makes honest she makes very ill-favoredly." If Mrs. Arnold had been old and plain, things might have assumed a different aspect. But what chiefly influences me as to her guilt is the inherent improbability. To suppose that the British would have actually carried on such dangerous negotiations through a flighty girl of twenty is absurd The most that can be imagined is that Arnold told her everything. But Arnold was a middle-aged man of vast experience. Franks testified specifically that Mrs. Arnold "was subject to occasional paroxysms of physical indisposition, attended by nervous debility, during which she would give utterance to anything and everything on her mind. This was a fact well known among us of the general's family; so much as to cause us to be scrupulous of what we told her or said within her hearing." [23] Who can believe that her husband would have confided weighty matters to a woman of that type? He would rather have said, with Macbeth,

> "Be innocent of the knowledge, dearest chuck,
> Till thou applaud the deed."

The one thing to be emphasized, which is generally overlooked, is that, if Mrs. Arnold had been cognizant of what was going on, her measure of guilt would have been totally different from his. She was a child, who had probably grown up to adore British uniforms and British society. Neither politics nor military loyalty would have meant anything to her. Her husband had been abused and persecuted and was at last restoring his allegiance where it belonged. The rest would have been detail.

70

1 of 1

And from such a point of view her complicity would
have been comparatively excusable, if it were psy-
chologically possible at all.

I do not think it was, more, at any rate, than
as a matter of constant, instinctive wifely pressure,
if it was even that. Arnold's financial situation
and his wounded pride furnish ample motives for
his conduct, without resorting to Mrs. Arnold.
And evidently her countrymen, from Washington down, were disposed to exonerate her. Otherwise she would hardly have been permitted to return
safely to Philadelphia, or to reside there, even for a
time. This she did. After a few weeks, however,
people began to get restive over the presence of the
wife of an avowed enemy, and in spite of Mrs.
Arnold's offer to break off all relations with her
husband, she was compelled to leave Philadelphia
and take refuge with Arnold in New York.

III

After a stay of a year in that city Mrs. Arnold
went with her husband to England, and from that
time England was her home, except for a brief
visit to her relatives in Philadelphia, when it appears that she was somewhat coldly received by
society at large, and an also brief residence at St.

John, New Brunswick, where her husband had some property. During the years in England, till her death in 1804, she kept up an active correspondence with her father and others, and from this we are able to get an accurate and varied insight into her character.

It is clear that she was by nature distinctly social. Human interests, human contact, the movement and activity of the great world, meant life to her, and it was mainly as she felt these that she was conscious of living herself. There is no evidence that she was abnormally dependent upon admiration or attention, or that she had the least tendency toward unfeeling coquetry. No doubt she was aware of her singular beauty, and no doubt she enjoyed the consideration it brought her, both in earlier years and even later. She would have been poorly woman if she had not. But scandal does not seem to have touched her, and her social interest was simply the strong spontaneous human instinct which is the most potent and satisfactory agent for holding society together. She liked to meet people; she liked to hear about people, their personal concerns and daily doings; she liked to play a considerable part in the doings of the world. It is true that at one time, under stress of circumstances, she declares, "my ambition has sunk with my fortune," [24]

72

but later it springs up again, and she refers charmingly to "my vanity, or the natural ambition, which I confess has often annoyed me." [25]

This social and human interest is the more striking in Mrs. Arnold, because there seems to be a conspicuous absence of some other elements. In her very extensive correspondence there is no allusion whatever to books; the intellectual side of life seems left out altogether. Religion is there in decent degree. Almighty God is a social personage who should be considered, like George the Third; but the search for Him is not a passion in her life. As to the country, no. Her father mildly suggests living there; it might be cheaper.[26] But rural economy and solitude do not appeal. "The country in England with a certain establishment is delightful; but to go into it with a confined income, unknown and unable to associate with the most respectable part of its inhabitants, would be extremely painful to me and would be too lonely for either my dear girl, or myself." [27] The notion of associating with trees and flowers and birds would be ridiculous. They have not clothes or manners or distinction, or even souls, and what would life be if one could not mix with these?

Nevertheless, it hardly seems that in England the social ambition was much gratified. In spite of the patronage of the king and of a few persons of importance, English society in general did not greatly relish Arnold's past history and kept aloof from him. The isolation that resulted is pathetically indicated in Mrs. Arnold's complaint, during one of her husband's absences, of being "in a strange country, without a creature near me that is really interested in my fate." [28] It might be supposed that such charm as is manifested in the Lawrence portrait would have attracted admiration and sympathy. No doubt it did; but it takes more than a pretty face to break down the barriers of English society. In this connection I hope the reader will enjoy as I do another of our biographer's delightful deductions. He quotes the assertion of a contemporary, that Mrs. Arnold was "the handsomest woman in England," couples it with her own statement that she feared she might lose the pension which had been granted her by George the Third, because she had no influence with his successor, and then infers that as the handsomest woman in England was not the mistress of the regent she must have been virtuous.[29] I do not require this evidence of Mrs. Arnold's virtue, but I do much appreciate the exhibition of logical agility.

Mrs. Arnold's intelligence may not have been largely cultivated in abstract lines, but no one can deny that she was quick, active, and energetic in practical matters. All her life she had sensitive nerves to fight against, and when the struggle with circumstances came hardest, she was apt to have internal difficulties to contend with, as well as external. In the crisis at West Point she was said to have been hysterical to the verge of actual delirium. In a later crisis in England she herself writes that "for some hours my reason was despaired of." [30] After Arnold's death in 1801 she was in a state of extreme nervous depression, even amounting to "a total loss of memory as far as relates to present occurrences." [31] Yet there was the element of reserve, by which such high-strung temperaments somehow keep a hold upon themselves when it is absolutely necessary. A friend speaks of her having "that fortitude and resignation which in a superior and well-regulated mind *only* is capable of existing," [32] and there is no question but that she had and displayed these excellent qualities. It is clear that she directed her household and her household affairs with skill, prudence, and success.

It is particularly interesting to follow her in money matters, for what concerns a wife and mother more vitally than this? Mrs. Arnold has been often accused of extravagance. It is urged that her taste for expenditure and display was a

main cause of her husband's financial troubles and
hence of his ruin. Here again the faithful biographer does not fail her. Extravagant? Of course
she was not extravagant. Over and over in her
letters she insists upon the necessity of economy
and her immense and constant efforts to exercise it.
She wishes to do the best she can for her children,
to give them every possible advantage, "always
keeping in view the absolute necessity of living
within my little income." [33] Her father especially
commends her discretion, and in good set terms declares that "I never had reason to distrust your
prudence." [34]

Which is all perfectly just. Only, it is quite possible to be well aware of the value of money and
of one's limitations in regard to it, and still to spend
very freely. There are, of course, those who squan-
der with no discretion, and it cannot be for a moment maintained that Mrs. Arnold belonged to the
number. But perhaps the most fundamental distinction in money concerns is between those who
want little and those who want a great deal. It is
only the former who are really independent finan-
cially and can afford to treat money as an indifferent matter. And Mrs. Arnold did not belong
to this class. She liked pretty clothes: "If anything very new and elegant is to be bought, that

you think I should like, pray purchase it for me." [35]
She liked comfort and ease and the good things of
the world that are at once indispensable and almost
negative to those who are used to them. Above all,
she liked to make a good showing before society,
to keep up appearances. A carriage, she must have
a carriage: "The want of a carriage I shall most
feel, not only in point of comfort, but respectability.
I have been endeavoring so to economize as to enable me with prudence to keep one for three or
four months in the winter." [36] She was used to
living like a lady, with ladies, and she could not bear
not to do it, and it is amazing how much being a lady
costs: "I am almost sick of the struggle to keep up
an appearance, which, however, is absolutely necessary, in this country, to bring forward a young
family." [37] When you like so many things that cost
money, you are pretty sure to spend it.

Yet, although she might feel inclined or obliged
to spend, it is clear that Mrs. Arnold knew the value
of money, how to handle it and to make it go far.
Also, she was a woman of business to a surprising
extent. She gave a great deal of shrewd and careful thought to the subject of investments, exercised
elaborate foresight as to the future, and her letters
to and from her father are full of minute discussion
of business matters. Besides her pension from the

Crown, she had property of her own, and few could better have understood the management of it. She was intimately conversant with her husband's rather complicated dealings, and clearly disapproved of his speculative tendencies, though, like many other people, not unwilling to profit by them, when there were any profits. After his death she set herself with extraordinary energy to the task, which would have burdened a man of business, of clearing up the tangled relics of his estate, and the self-satisfaction with which she recounts her efforts is not only pardonable, but delightful: "I have paid every *ascertained* debt due from the estate of my late lamented husband, within four or five hundred pounds, and this I have the means of discharging. I will not attempt to describe to you the toil it has been to me; but may without vanity add, that few women could have effected what I have done." [38]

IV

Mrs. Arnold's relations with the various members of her family, as fully developed in her letters, are always charming. Her affection for her father, and his for her, are peculiarly constant and significant. He writes to her at great length, expressing the deepest solicitude for her welfare, extending advice and more substantial assistance in liberal measure. When her husband's death and her own ill-health bring endless trouble upon her, the father deeply regrets that his age and his burdens make it impossible for him to cross the ocean to console her. And after her death he expressed to one of her English friends his solemn assurance that "her well-spent life will secure her a happy existence hereafter." [39]

The daughter's letters are equally tender and responsive. She longs to visit her parent, longs to give him the care and attention which his age should receive from her, to talk over her difficulties and get the benefit of his counsel. The feeling with which she acknowledges the gift of his picture is touching in its tender intensity: "The sight of it occasioned sensations I never before experienced; and though I scarcely had it out of my hand the whole of the day I received it, I could not rest without getting up twice in the night to look at it," [40] which is surely a testimony of affection that ought to appeal to anyone.

Margaret's letters to her sisters are also attractive, full at once of cordial confidence and natural interest in family and friendly matters. Nor is she less sisterly or less dignified in her references to the brother who seems to have got into financial difficulties and to have entangled her affairs with his own. But what puzzles me, as I have indicated earlier, is the slight appearance of the mother in all this correspondence. She lived till 1794, that is for thirteen years after Margaret went to England. Yet during all that time we are given no single letter addressed to her. Her husband speaks of her with much tenderness and deplores her death as an infinite loss. Margaret occasionally refers to her mother's health and inquires for her with respect; but there is no evidence of the dependence or intimate longing which one would have expected to find. What does it mean, as regards Margaret, or her mother, or both? I wish I knew.

With her own immediate family Mrs. Arnold is as interesting and as dutiful as with her relatives at home. Arnold had sons by his former marriage who were brought up by his sister. With the sister, who seems to have been an admirable woman, Mrs. Arnold was on most friendly terms, and for the sons she showed exceptional consideration, thoughtfulness, and a really exquisite desire to do what was in every way fair and loyal. She looked after their material needs, advised them in their difficulties, and particularly mediated between them and their father when there was occasion for doing so. "My conduct," she wrote them after Arnold's death, "has been dictated by regard to you, respect to your dear father's memory, and an earnest desire to act with uprightness, feeling, and tenderness." [41] There is every reason to believe that she did act so throughout.

With her own children, above all, Mrs. Arnold was charming, all that a mother could be asked to be. She enjoyed them when well, she tended them when ill, and when she was ill herself, her dread of being a burden to them was so great and her desire to spare them so intense that, in her abnormal state of mind, it almost drove her to suicide: "At one period, when I viewed everything through a false medium, I fancied that nothing but the sacrifice of my life would benefit my children, for that my wretchedness embittered every moment of their lives; and dreadful to say, I was many times on the point of making the sacrifice." [42]

She had one daughter, Sophia, and four sons. All the effort of her life was directed to getting these children on in the world and to giving them such training as would enable them to fill a distinguished station with credit and success. Here again, as is natural, the substance of her own ambition is reflected in her ambition for them. There is no hint of any intellectual pursuit or interest, or that any such thing as books existed in the world. There is no special insistence on religious influence, or de-

WIVES

sire that the children should do good or live to
benefit their fellow men. Public positions, prominence in the army or navy or political life, social
success and standing, supported by the solid goods
of fortune and also of character, these were the sort
of things that the mother had always wished for
herself. Why should she wish anything else for her
children?

And her wishes were gratified, and that they
were so must, no doubt, as usual, be attributed
mainly to her effort and devotion. Her children
seem all to have been profoundly attached to her,
and she speaks repeatedly of the comfort they
bring her, of her pride in them, and of the absence
of anything in their conduct to cause her regret.
"But when I assert that two of my sons have arrived at the age of manhood without having by
any misconduct given me an hour's uneasiness; and
that my third son is exactly treading in their steps,
you will not think it a vain boast, when I do justice to their worth." [43] If you consider how one
hundred millions of Americans feel about Benedict
Arnold, it is interesting that their mother could so
speak of his sons.

v

For they were the sons of Benedict Arnold, and
she was Benedict Arnold's wife, and no other phase

82

of her career is so curious to study as her relation to him. First, one is curious as to his feeling about her; but indications on this point are difficult to come across. What is most striking in Arnold's English years is his silence. We have not one really personal word to show us what he felt about anything. Regret, remorse, explanation, apology, ambition, hope for the future, nothing comes to us. For twenty long years the man's soul is practically hidden behind the curtain of oblivion, and it is hardly to be expected that such a minor element as marital love should be more elaborately revealed than other things. In the earlier period there are gleams of tenderness. Hannah Arnold, his sister, writes to Margaret during her husband's absence: "Yesterday got a letter from your anxious husband, who, lover-like, is tormenting himself with a thousand fancied disasters which have happened to you and the family." [44] Again, Arnold sends to his wife in Philadelphia minute directions for her journey to join him at West Point, which show a very attractive and considerate solicitude: "Let me beg of you not to make your stages so long as to fatigue yourself or the dear boy." [45] At the very end we have Arnold's will, "I give and bequeath to my beloved wife . . . all my estate both *real* and *personal* . . . to be disposed of among *all* my children at her death, as she may think proper, not doubting her doing them all equal justice." [46] And Mrs. Arnold is made sole executrix, which is perhaps as solid a proof of trust and affection as one can ask for. But with this more remote and formal testimony we have to be content, so far as Arnold himself is concerned.

The industrious biographer, always watchful and always logical, makes one of his remarkable inferences from a late letter of Mrs. Arnold's: "I sometimes fear that my reason will give way.—My sufferings are not of the present moment only.—Years of unhappiness have passed, I had cast my lot, complaints were unavailing, and you and my other friends are ignorant of the many causes of uneasiness I have had." [47] This, says the biographer, means "the painful discovery that although her happiness had been sacrificed for Arnold, yet he had not always remained true to her." [48] What unerring vision some persons are gifted with! That Arnold was faithful I should gravely doubt, considering his character and his past; but I should want more evidence than the above to assert the contrary. At any rate, his wife does not hesitate elsewhere to speak of him as "the best of husbands" [49] and to deplore "the loss of a husband

whose affection for me was unbounded." [50] I believe
it was, as it certainly ought to have been.

For her tenderness and devotion to him appear
in all her letters, though we have not a single word
addressed to him directly. When he is absent, she
longs for him and cannot be at rest till she knows
where he is and how he does. She hears of the capture of a town where he is supposed to be and
writes passionately that till she gets definite word
she "shall not know a moment's peace of mind." [51]
But the most interesting and striking display of
her feelings occurs in connection with the duel
fought by Arnold with Lord Lauderdale, because
the latter had made insinuations with regard to
Arnold's conduct in America, Mrs. Arnold became
aware of what was impending before the duel occurred and she describes minutely her sufferings in
connection with it. Anxious as she was, she yet
thought first of what was due to her husband's
reputation: "Weak woman as I am, I would not
wish to prevent what would be deemed necessary
to preserve his honor." [52] Yet the strain was hardly
endurable: "What I suffered for near a week is
not to be described: the suppression of my feelings,
lest I should unman the general, almost at last
proved too much for me; and for some hours my
reason was despaired of." [53] When all ends well

and Lord Lauderdale calls upon her, to express "concern at finding that I had been made unhappy," and some of the first characters in the kingdom visit the general to applaud his procedure, she has this charming word of appreciation of herself: "Nor am I displeased at the great commendations bestowed on my own conduct upon this trying occasion." [54]

She loved him, there is no doubt about that. But through it all, the question that teases me is, what she thought of him. That is always the puzzle with wives. With husbands, also, you say. Well, yes. But husbands are more often busy and indifferent. They take the wife and her affection for granted, and go bustle about the world's affairs. But the wife has—or had, in the older time—secluded hours and days and years. Her husband is, after all, pretty much the whole of life to her. She knows him, at any rate, vastly better than anyone else does. She judges him, criticizes him, appreciates every little foible, oh, not in definite words, perhaps, even to herself; but she knows, all the same, she has to know, to adapt her life and all her conduct and even her thoughts to those foibles. Yet to get her judgment and her intimate knowledge is always a difficult and often an impossible task. The instant anyone else judges or criticizes, she leaps to defend, not so much him, but herself, her judgment, her choice, her love. If you want to get the truth, you have to watch, to divine, to develop, with the subtlest care.

Such a process is immensely difficult when, as with Mrs. Arnold, we have only indirect and more or less formal correspondence. As to the one central event of Arnold's career, it may be said at once that we have no word from her at all. What she thought of it we can only guess in the obscurest way. As to his later life, what is most interesting and impressive is her obstinate effort to defend his reputation, to see that his name was transmitted to his children without a stain or blot upon it, and does not this show that she did not for a moment recognize anything reprehensible in his earlier conduct? Or does it? To pay his debts, to assure his respectable standing in the world, for this she toiled with incessant, unfailing loyalty, and, it might almost be said, laid down her life. "I have rescued your father's memory from disrespect by paying all his just debts, and his children will now never have the mortification of being reproached with his speculations having injured anybody beyond his own family; and his motives, not the unfortunate termination, will be considered by them, and his memory will be doubly dear to them." [55] His motives, not the unfortunate termination—was it not thus she looked at his whole career? As she expresses it elsewhere, in connection with a specific instance, but I think certainly with a general bearing: "The solicitude was in itself so praiseworthy, and so disinterested, and never induced him to deviate from rectitude, that his children should ever reverence his memory." [56]

So the loyal wife asserts, and perhaps believes, that nothing ever induced her husband to deviate from rectitude, and that husband was Benedict Arnold. And what strikes one most in it all is the frightful, desperate solidarity of husband and wife, through heaven and hell. The woman was delightful, adorable, and ought to have been remembered as such. Yet the one thing that causes her to linger in history is that she was the wife of a traitor. You may extenuate, you may mitigate, emphasize her innocence, her grace, her tenderness, her nobility, her charm; but always, when she is spoken of, comes, "Oh, the wife of the traitor, Arnold." What strange, involving, enduring perdition we unwittingly bring upon ourselves!

IV

THEODOSIA BURR

CHRONOLOGY

Theodosia Burr Alston.
Born, Albany, June 23, 1783.
Mother died, 1794.
Married Joseph Alston, February 2, 1801.
Son died, June 30, 1812.
Died at sea, January, 1813.

THEODOSIA BURR

I

CONSIDERING that women in general are not sea-farers and that their perils and disasters are rather of a domestic order, it is curious that two of the most notable, brilliant, and interesting figures among American women, Margaret Fuller and Theodosia Burr, should have been lost at sea.

But indeed Theodosia's life was picturesque, sudden, and tumultuous in every way. Her distinguished, disreputable father said of himself, "It seems I must always move in a whirlwind."[1] Theodosia wrote: "What a charming thing a bustle is! Oh, dear, delightful confusion! It gives a circulation to the blood, an activity to the mind, and a spring to the spirits."[2] If bustle was what she liked, she got it. She was the great-granddaughter of Jonathan Edwards, and no doubt she received so much of his pious inheritance as her father had not frittered away. Born in 1783, before the new American nation had settled down, she lost her mother when she was ten years old, and her existence became involved in the eccentric orbit of her father's fortunes. She watched him first in the hurly burly of New York politics, then she saw him become Vice-President of the United States in 1800, then he was thrown into disgrace by the duel with Hamilton in 1804. Meantime, at seventeen, she had married a wealthy South Carolina planter, Joseph Alston, who later became Governor of the State, and she swung back and forth between her father in New York and her Southern home. Then in 1806 Burr developed his wild dream of a Spanish-American empire. Theodosia shared it, and visited the victimized Blennerhassetts on their exquisite island in the Ohio River. Her father was arrested and tried in Richmond for treason. She shared that episode also. Then he went abroad for four years, practically in exile, and she longed for him and labored for him with passionate ardor, though her affections were also absorbed by the husband and the one boy at home. Just as her father at last achieved his return, she lost the boy, and her life seemed wrecked forever. On the last day but one of 1812, when she was twenty-nine years old, she sailed from Charleston to meet her father in New York, and was never definitely heard of again. It does not require mythical pirates, who drowned her, to complete the tragedy.[3] Surely by that time the poor child had had bustle enough and would have relished the lovely epitaph which Byron found in an Italian cemetery—*implora eterna pace.*

Theodosia's mother was a delightful woman, and her influence on the child's earlier years must not be overlooked. Her maiden name was De Visme and she was of Swiss origin, but she was a widow, Mrs. Prevost, with two children, when Burr married her, and it should be said that Burr always treated these children with consideration and tenderness. His wife's devotion to him is one of the assets in Burr's singular career, for it is evident from her letters that she was a woman of unusual nobility and charm. That she loved him as long as she lived, with a girlish abandon, is clear enough: "I am impatient for the evening; for the receipt of your dear letter; for those delightful sensations which your expressions of tenderness alone can excite. Dejected, distracted without them, elated. giddy even to folly with them, my mind, never at medium, claims everything from your partiality." [4] Yet she was by no means an emotional or capricious creature. On the contrary, her letters show a most apt and responsive intelligence, always improving itself and on the watch for the curious and helpful lessons of the world. She read widely. In one letter

93

Burr recommends to her Plutarch, Herodotus, Gibbon, and Plautus for light reading,[5] and I have no doubt she turned to the books for themselves as well as for him.

In view of the wide later ambitions of her husband and daughter, it is interesting to observe that Mrs. Burr was not without her frank confession of interest in the upward efforts of the world. In speaking of the Empress Catherine of Russia she says: "What a glorious figure will she make on the historical page! Can you form an idea of a more happy mortal than she will be when seated on the throne of Constantinople? How her ambition will be gratified!"[6] To such an ardent spirit a mythical throne in Mexico might have had a certain appeal. Yet what is most striking about Mrs. Burr is her earnestness and loftiness of moral tone. Whatever her husband may have been, she was consistently noble and high-minded, and her religion, though probably not narrow or dogmatical, was pervasive and sincere. "Piety teaches resignation. . . . The better I am acquainted with it, the more charms I find. Worlds should not purchase the little I possess. I promise myself many happy hours dedicated at the shrine of religion."[7]

That this lady kept a close and careful watch on her daughter's education we may take for

THEODOSIA BURR

granted, but there is less evidence of the mother's control than of the father's, because, owing to his frequent absence, his interest was expressed in letters that have come down to us. It may be said at once that few fathers manifest not only a more affectionate, but a more intelligent and judicious care of their children's welfare and spiritual and intellectual progress. Burr was unquestionably lawless in his dealings with women but he never had a contempt for them. Above all, he was in advance of his time in his belief that woman's brain was capable of as much as man's and should be given the same culture and nourishment.[8] He was determined that his daughter at least should not be turned over to the frivolities and drawing-room accomplishments which were then considered all that was necessary for her sex. She was to study serious subjects and to master them—mathematics, sciences, history, languages, literature; he advises her as to all of them, and sees that she keeps at it and makes progress. When one thinks of what he himself was, and what his life had been and was about to be, one sometimes gasps at the quality of the advice which he pours out so freely; but taken in itself, it is excellent and might well produce the best results, even if the source was somewhat tainted: "Not that the languages alone can decide your happiness or mine; but if you should abandon the attempt, or despair of success, or relax your endeavors, it would indicate a feebleness of character which would dishearten me exceedingly." [9] Again, "Negligence of one's duty produces a self-dissatisfaction which unfits the mind for everything, and ennui and peevishness are the never-failing consequences. You will readily discover the truth of these remarks by reflecting on your own conduct, and the different feelings which have flowed from a persevering attention to study, or a restless neglect of it." [10]

As a result of these paternal efforts, Theodosia used her intelligence faithfully and zealously all her brief life; and the intelligence was evidently clear, acute, and penetrating. The reading which her father prescribed for her was somewhat remarkable. She seems to have studied both Latin and Greek at an early age. When she was ten years old, her father writes, "I am sure you will be charmed with the Greek language above all others," [11] and a few months later he remonstrates against the neglect of Greek verbs.[12] He recommends the Odyssey, recommends Terence, and when she is married and a busy mother, he hopes she reads "Quintilian in the original, and not in translation." [13] And Theodosia's own letters are not without allusions to the authors that she loves. Perhaps she may have had a little more leaning to the romantic and frivolous than her father would have approved; but, if so, he had succeeded bravely in eradicating it, and by the time she was twenty she had eschewed light fiction as unprofitable: "Novel-reading has, I find, not only the ill effect of rendering people romantic, which, thanks to my father on earth, I am long past, but they really furnish no occupation to the mind. A series of events follow so rapidly, and are interwoven with remarks so commonplace and so spun out, that there is nothing left to reflect upon." [14] With a mind so well equipped and so active, it would seem natural that Theodosia should have attempted writing, and if she had lived I imagine she would have done so. As it is, there is nothing of the kind but her charming letters and a project of translation which was never carried out.[15]

It must not be supposed, however, that the girl was a pedant or a blue-stocking. She was thoroughly feminine in her tastes and instincts, enjoyed society, and was fitted to shine in it. She was lovely to look at, with a strangely simple, round, baby face, but clearly intelligent and sensitive. There is no sign that she was coquettish or over-fanciful in her dress; but she liked pretty things, and liked to

display them: "You must send me the shawl. I shall
be down at the races, and want to have the gratification of displaying it." [16] How charming is her
appeal to her father about her appearance at a
party: "I danced twice, but I am unable to tell
you whether I looked well or danced well; for you
are the only person in the world who says anything to me about my appearance. *Mari* generally
looks pleased, but rarely makes remarks." [17]

Indeed, as in intellectual, so in social, education,
the father was the trusted adviser and guide. And,
on the whole, it must be said that his counsel here
too was excellent. There are times when it savors
a little of his admired Chesterfield, as when Theodosia visits an old lady who likes to see children
fed frugally, and he urges her to be very sparing of
meat and drink, for the sake of the good impression. If a reason is asked, she is to say, *Papa thinks
it not good for me.*[18] But in the main his precepts
are as kindly and human as they are wise. She is to
seek the society of her fellows and not avoid it; she
is to be careful not to bore anyone; she is to understand, to sympathize, to learn to bear the little rubs
and vexations without annoyance: "Let me tell you
that you will always feel much better, much hap-
pier, for having borne with serenity the spleen of
anyone, than if you had returned spleen for

spleen."[19] Above all, he begs her to cultivate the appearance of cheerfulness and kindliness, well appreciating that the substance is bound to be developed by the manifestation, and I do not know what saner social counsel could come from any source: "There is nothing more certain than that you may form what countenance you please. An open, serene, intelligent countenance, a little brightened by cheerfulness, not wrought into smiles or simpers, will presently become familiar and grow into habit. . . . Avoid, forever avoid, a smile or sneer of contempt; never even mimic them. A frown of sullenness or discontent is but one degree less hateful."[20] It is easy to understand that the man who formed his conduct on such a principle was one of the most beloved, as well as hated, of his generation.

His daughter was beloved also. Such expressions as we have about her are quite ecstatic in their enthusiasm. Even Blennerhassett, who detested her father and her husband, says of himself and of that strange Luther Martin who defended Burr in his trial, "I also find his idolatrous admiration of Mrs. Alston is almost as excessive as my own."[21] And Mrs. Blennerhassett goes further still: "I should not think my life even worth its present value, did not I hope once more to see and converse with that woman whom I think almost above human nature." [22] Theodosia's own expressions of friendship show that this popularity was founded on a singular tenderness and power of delicate apprehension and comprehension. [23]

Unfortunately, circumstances contributed too much to blight these gentler feelings. The disgrace which overtook her father reacted largely upon Theodosia's own social prospects and surroundings, and she was forced to recognize the shallowness of much of the world's affection and the bitter lining of its apparent kindliness and grace. Acquaintances fell off from her, friends neglected her: "Mrs. —— had even the cruelty to tell me that I had been so long ill and so long friendless, that I could not feel as keenly as others would; and if I did, I should have remained at home; not moved about the world helpless and dependent on others." [24] When such blows come, it is hard to keep the cheerful countenance, harder still the cheerful heart. Burr himself was born so infallibly gay that nothing could shake him. Friends might fail, hopes might wither, strength and means might vanish, he could still smile on. But his daughter was made of more delicate stuff, and it is clear that at times her eyes filled and her heart died within her.

How much religion did she have to strengthen

100

her? We do not know. Her father was pretty largely skeptical. One of her biographers insists that his skepticism was never allowed to affect her, that Burr kept it to himself. This I doubt. But, after all, his own skepticism was not violent and he regarded God with the same fine tolerance that he bestowed upon all animated beings. His is the truly admirable remark: "I think that God is a great deal better than people suppose." [25] On a brilliant summer night he wishes that he had his daughter with him to share his religious meditations: "I passed some hours on deck admiring the brilliancy of the stars, following their majestic march through infinite space, and tracing the hand of Omnipotence. Presumptuous aim! Yet there is a charm in such contemplations of which you know all the luxury. It is you only whose society I could endure on such occasions." [26]

As for Theodosia herself, we have hardly more than the exquisite words in regard to her husband and child, written when she thought she was dying, but I do not know that we could ask for anything more convincing or more lovely: "Oh, my heavenly Father, bless them both. If it is permitted, I will hover round and guard you, and intercede for you. I hope for happiness in the next world, for I have not been bad in this." [27]

II

These words are from a letter addressed to Theodosia's husband, and her husband of course played a conspicuous part of her life, though less so than he would have done if it had not been for her father. Joseph Alston was an important personage in South Carolina, belonged to a distinguished family, and had considerable possessions and abilities. Theodosia seems to have chosen him from affection, and there is a legend that she had earlier rejected Washington Irving.[28] But Alston's Southern life, habits, and tastes were naturally strange in many ways to a girl who had grown up in New York, and his wife did not always find it easy to adapt herself to them.

It would appear that Alston was an excellent man and an indulgent and devoted husband. We have intimate light on him from various quarters, which differs in quality, as might be expected. The Blennerhassetts, who were more or less involved with him in Burr's great Western conspiracy, naturally took an unfavorable view. Just how far Alston sympathized with his father-in-law's designs it is difficult to say, as indeed it is difficult to say what those designs were. But pressure like Theodosia's must have been hard to resist. Alston evidently admired Burr's brilliancy, and was no doubt taken with the glamor of his great adventure. He later denied complicity in any schemes against the government, but this did not mean much. At any rate, both Blennerhassett and his wife spoke harshly of him. "How can she live with such a man as Alston?" asks the lady. "You see he has not had humanity, or even politeness enough, to answer your letter." [29] Blennerhassett writes to his former confederate, accusing him of committing "the *shabby treason* of deserting from your parent by affinity, and your *sovereign* in *expectancy*." [30] On the other hand, Burr himself always refers to his son-in-law with affection and often with praise. In the farewell letter, written to Theodosia before the Hamilton duel, he suggests that Alston may write a sketch of his life and adds that "no one could do it so well as he." [31] Long after the date of the conspiracy he commends his son-in-law's military ability: "He has extraordinary talents in that line, and may never have another opportunity to display them." [32] It is only in moments of extreme anxiety as to Theodosia's health that he is disposed to criticize, and even then he is always ready to allow for the difficult circumstances with which the husband has to deal.

But we have not only the verdict of his associates

upon Alston's character, we have a number of his own letters, which bring out many of his traits in an interesting fashion. For example, there is the long and most curious epistle, written to Theodosia in the days of love-making, to overcome her objection to early marriages. It seems the young lady (at seventeen) had cited the august authority of Aristotle to the effect that "a man should not marry before he is six-and-thirty." The lover admits the weight of this learned opinion, but insists that even against Cicero, "who stands higher in my estimation than any other author," he cannot possibly accept her point of view. Early marriages are generally bad, no doubt; but his case is different. They are all always so touchingly different, aren't they? He is not a child. They never are. "Introduced from my infancy into the society of men, while yet a boy I was accustomed to think and act like a man. On every occasion, however important, I was left to decide for myself; I do not recollect a single instance where I was controlled even by advice; for it was my father's invariable maxim, that the best way of strengthening the judgment was to suffer it to be constantly exercised." [33] And, to be sure, at thirty-seven instead of seventeen, one might have stopped to wonder whether such a character was too well adapted to marriage at all, early or late. But

Theodosia was not thirty-seven, and she gave up Aristotle and consented.

And it is very clear that her husband retained his affection and admiration for her to the end. No doubt she was amply worthy of both. Still, one can see that he might have found some drawbacks. There is that terrible, engrossing, meteoric father. He played a great, strange part in the world, and also in Theodosia's life. It might easily be imagined that a husband would have found such a father difficult to put up with, might have been sometimes indignant with him and sometimes jealous of him. Perhaps Alston was both; probably he was. But nothing of it appears, even in the few of his own letters that we have or in the comments of either the father or the daughter. And what he writes to Burr, after Theodosia's death, certainly indicates the deepest and finest appreciation of all he had lost: "The talents of my boy, his rare elevation of character, his already extensive reputation for so early an age, made his death regretted by the pride of my family; but, though certain of the loss of my not less admirable wife, they seem to consider it like the loss of an ordinary woman. Alas! they know nothing of my heart. They never have known anything of it. Yet, after all, he is a poor actor who cannot sustain his little hour upon the stage, be his part what it may. But the man who has been deemed worthy of the heart of *Theodosia Burr,* and who has felt what it was to be blessed with such a woman's, will never forget his elevation." [34] And Alston gave the best testimony of his attachment by dying a few years after his wife and son, practically of a broken heart.

On Theodosia's affection for her husband we have much more vivid light than upon his for her. In the early days of her marriage, when she was absent in New York, she frequently wrote to him, and the letters have a charming touch of tenderness and grace: "Every moment I feel that I have lost so much of your society which can never be regained. Ah, my husband, what can be pleasure to your Theo., unassisted by the charms of your presence and participation? Nothing. It is an idea which has no place in my mind unconnected with you." [35] When he is ill, she writes: "You have been imprudent, and all my fears are fulfilled. Without anyone near you to feel for you, to attend to you, to watch every change and share every pain. Your wife only could do that. It is her whose soul clings to yours, and vibrates but in harmony with it; whose happiness, whose every emotion, more than entirely dependent on yours, are exchanged for them." [36]

The passage of years brought some rubs and

flaws in the beauty of this tenderness. Alas! it must be always so. These husbands perhaps live in the wilds of South Carolina, far from the sparkle and gayety of New York society. Again, these husbands have families, and sometimes it is wearing. Theodosia takes a journey with two of her husband's relatives, and the mischievous creature writes to her father: "We travel in company with the two Alstons. Pray teach me how to write two *A's* without producing something like an *Ass*." [37] Then there is always that father, and the strange complication that he makes of life, complication which is certainly enough to distract and terrify the best of husbands, so that there are times when it seems best to conceal one's doings from marital observation altogether. [38]

Yet there can be no doubt that Theodosia not only retained her husband's love to the end, but returned it to the full, and her influence over him must have been in proportion to the depth of their affection. The beautiful words of the farewell letter, from which I have already quoted, though written in 1805, would, I am sure, have been just as appropriate in 1812: "Death is not welcome to me. I confess it is ever dreaded. You have made me too fond of life. Adieu, then, thou kind, thou tender husband. Adieu, friend of my heart. May Heaven prosper you, and may we meet hereafter. . . . Least of all should I murmur. I, on whom so many blessings have been showered—whose days have been numbered by bounties—who have had such a husband, such a child, and such a father. . . . Adieu, once more, and for the last time, my beloved. Speak of me often to our son. Let him love the memory of his mother, and let him know how he was loved by her." [39]

III

As a housekeeper and mother, Theodosia, young as she was, seems to have borne herself with dignity and success. Her health was never robust, and the entirely new conditions with which her Southern married life was surrounded were not wholly favorable. Her father, who worries about so few things, worries constantly about her. When he is in Europe, he writes home with plans and suggestions. He urges attention and consideration upon her husband. And his nearest approach to temper is when he imagines Alston is neglecting his wife's welfare, and keeping her in South Carolina when she should be transported to New York: "He gave me his word before marriage, and I claim now the renewal of that promise. You may be made to do anything;

to say anything; to write anything. After four experiments, all nearly fatal, I would not have made *a fifth with a dog.*" [40] Theodosia herself, when she is ill, turns to the thought of her father for comfort, and longs for his advice.[41] There are times when continued and prospective weakness depresses and discourages her. But it is evident that she was not one of those who cherish imaginary symptoms, or count on an enfeebled condition to create sympathy: "I exert myself to the utmost, feeling none of that pride so common to my sex, of being weak and ill." [42] When effort was called for, she displayed it, and she clearly had the gift of getting things done. Her father is impressed with the rapidity with which her "house has been furnished and established," [43] and calls her husband's attention to it. And the daughter quietly and simply states her view of the way in which life ought to be met and dealt with: "In running away from duties, there is something cowardly which I never could bear." [44]

There is one point on which I wish I had more light, and that is Theodosia's management of money. Did she share her father's incurable thriftlessness, her father who gayly wrote of himself, "I never buy a bit of furniture or take the smallest trip without being duped and plundered; and, when it is past, I console myself with the experience I have gained, and the full assurance that it is the very last time; and this has gone on pretty much the same way near forty years." [45] Was Theodosia affected by what may be called the reaction of alternate generations, through which we so often see a child instinctively avoiding the weaknesses and excesses of its parent, perhaps even falling into an opposite excess? Certainly the daughter in this case had no trace of narrowness or meanness, but I cannot help thinking that hard experience in childhood had taught her something more of prudence and forethought than her father ever learned. At any rate, she bewails his European poverty and makes desperate, if not very successful, efforts to relieve it.

Whatever her economic abilities, she undoubtedly had occasion for them in running her establishment, which must have been at all times a considerable one. Alston had the slaves, the general equipment, and the elaborate, as well as primitive, living arrangements of a Southern planter, and Theodosia, at seventeen, had to go in and take charge of these, and I have no question but that she did it, and did it well. She had always been accustomed to a similar elaborateness in her father's house, however great may have been the uncertainty of paying for it. This well appears in Burr's account of his preparation for one of her visits: "Of horses I have five; three always and wholly at your devotion, and the whole five occasionally. Harry and Sam are both good coachmen, either at your orders. Of servants there are enough for family purposes. Eleonore, however, must attend you, for the sake of the heir apparent. You will want no others, as there are at my house Peggy, Nancy, and a small girl of about eleven. Mr. Alston may bring a footman. Anything further will be useless; he may, however, bring six or eight of them, if he like." [46] While another brief passage, with its charming suggestion of "bustle," gives a vivid picture of the state in which Mrs. Alston traveled: "Heigho! for Richmond Hill. What a pity you were not here, you do so love a bustle; and then you, and the brat, and the maid, and thirty trunks would add so charmingly to the confusion." [47]

In her attitude towards her little son Theodosia is as faithful as she is attractive. Her letters to her father are full of the child, though not more so than her father's to her. Burr adored his grandson and namesake and poured out incessant counsels and suggestions as to his education. Tutors? He must have the best tutors, must be taught languages, and mathematics, and literature. His mother must keep at him, and if she does not, must be scolded: "If you had one particle of invention or genius, you would have taught A. B. A. his *a, b, c* before this. God mend you. His fibbing is an inheritance, which pride, an inheritance, will cure. His mother went through that process." [48] Burr wants him taught energy also, outdoor sports, and some contact with life, such as is essential to fit him for success in a democracy. [49] When the child, at four years old, meets an infuriated goat and puts him to flight with a stick, the grandfather's soldier-heart is entirely delighted. [50]

And Theodosia listens quietly to all this paternal advice, and takes it in, and profits by it. But it is quite clear that she manages her child in her own way, and intends to do so, probably in thoughtful consultation with his father. She superintends his lessons, superintends his morals, watches over his health, wants him to be a man, and a brave one, and a good one. How pretty is her anxiety when on some trifling occasion of alarm the boy is terrified and runs to her and catches her skirts. "Do you think this trait ominous of a coward? You know my abhorrence and contempt of those animals. Really I have been uneasy ever since it happened." [51]

But through the anxiety and discipline it is evident how much she loved him. And then he died, was snatched away from her just when she had enshrined all her hope in him, and all her pride, and all her life. The two letters written to her father, shortly after the loss, are tragic in their dry-eyed misery, their quiet revelation of a spiritual universe in ruins. "Alas! my dear father, I do live, but how does it happen? Of what am I formed that I live, and why? Of what service can I be in this world, either to you or anyone else, with a body reduced to premature old age, and a mind enfeebled and bewildered? . . . Whichever way I turn, the same anguish still assails me. You talk of consolation. Ah! you know not what you have lost. I think Omnipotence could give me no equivalent for my boy; no, none—none."[52] And again I turn back to that pathetic farewell letter, written years before, when she had no thought that the child's death would precede hers, and it is touching to see the three strands of interwoven love, which made up all her life, so closely mingled together: "Let my father see my son sometimes. Do not be unkind towards him whom I have loved so much, I beseech you. . . . Adieu, my sweet boy. Love your father; be grateful and affectionate to him while he lives; be the pride of his meridian, the support of his departing days. Be all that he wishes; for he made your mother happy."[53]

IV

But, interesting as Theodosia was in her relations to her husband and her son, it is unquestionably the relation to her father that is the predominant and most impressive thing in her life.

As to Burr's worship of her there can be no doubt whatever, and it is the finest and most attractive element in his chequered character and career. I have already indicated his solicitude for her education in her youth and for her health at all times. But his attention and absorption appear everywhere in his letters and journals. He writes before her marriage: "The happiness of my life depends on your exertions; for what else, for whom else do I live?" [54] During the lonely years of his European exile his heart turns to her with a clinging tenderness that is singularly touching in its entire simplicity of expression. "I am always full of trouble at the moment of despatching letters, being always a little too late, of which you have had too many examples. It is only to you, however. My letters to others are always ready; but towards you, a desire to say something at the last moment—a reluctance resembling that of parting; but all this you know and feel." [55] If he has sudden hopes of fortune, if his wild speculations for once promise to turn out well, the instant thought is that he can

114

do much for her: "If I can get a passport to Bremen and Amsterdam, I will send you·a million of francs within six months; but one half of it must be laid out in pretty things. Oh, what beautiful things I will send you." [56] When the direst poverty presses him, the very last resort is to sell the precious keepsakes that were hers: "The money must be raised or the voyage given up. So, after turning it over, and looking at it, and opening it, and putting it to my ear like a baby, and kissing it, and begging you a thousand pardons out loud, your dear, little beautiful watch was—was sold." [57] The final disaster of her death did more to shatter his extraordinary equanimity than anything else that ever happened to him, and though he lived on for many years, and loved and laughed and spent and trifled, the scar on his heart was never quite obliterated.

What is perhaps most singular about this paternal tenderness is the utter confidence of self-revelation in it. There seems to have been no fold of his subtle and complicated spirit that this man was not ready to open before the child whom he adored. There was no reluctance, there was no modesty, there was no shame. Few men would think of writing to their sons as he writes to this high-minded and exquisite daughter. All his love-affairs and projects of remarriage are submitted to her criticism and comment. When he thinks that death may result from the duel with Hamilton, he wishes her to burn all of his letters which, if by any accident made public, would injure any person: "This is more particularly applicable to the letters of my female correspondents." [58] Above all, when he was in Europe he kept a minute daily diary, which was confessedly intended to be perused by Theodosia, and to form notes for future talks with her. Again and again she expresses her delight at the thought of seeing it.[59] Yet there are few more scandalous records of erotic adventure extant anywhere. Can you imagine Pepys keeping his diary expressly to be shown to his daughter? But that is apparently what Burr did. Biographers have attempted to get rid of the difficulty by suggesting that he merely sent her an expurgated copy. This may be true. But in one passage at least he requests her to refer to her copy to verify some incident as if there were no other in existence.[60] And any such labor of duplication seems very unlike Burr, while the tone of the whole implies the image of Theodosia looking over his shoulder when he wrote it. The only possible solution of the puzzle lies in the extraordinary temper of the man, his combination of an extreme subtlety and sophistication with a childlike naïveté, such as we see so often exemplified in the elder

116

Dumas. But even so, it is a singular spiritual phenomenon, both for him and for her.

At any rate, as a result of so much confidence and affection, he acquired a very great influence over her. It is touching and beautiful to see how she turns to him for advice and guidance in every crisis of her life. In one of the most curious passages in his letters he shows how great he himself felt this influence to be. "From any man save one, if I cannot vanquish, I can escape. In the hands of that one, I am just what Theodosia is in mine. This was perceived after the first two hours; and seeing no retreat, nor anything better to be done, I surrendered, tame and unresisting, to be disarmed, stripped, hacked, hewed, dissected, skinned, turned inside out, at the will and mercy of the operator." [61]

Nevertheless, I cannot help feeling that he somewhat overrated his power, at least that in reality the daughter's was the stronger nature of the two, that when she was really convinced, she went her way, with true feminine persistency, and even that perhaps in the end she swayed him more than he did her. See what she says as to one decision: "All I can add in writing is, that my judgment approves. If yours does not, I can only bewail a destiny which places me amid so many contending duties; surrenders up my heart a victim to such various feelings, and at length robs me of that serenity which is deemed the infallible reward of sacrificing pleasure to what is right in our own estimation." [62] She advises him almost like an older sister in his matrimonial perplexities, and it is evident that he wants her advice and takes it. With what a noble cry does she stimulate him to endeavor and to hope: "Tell me that you are engaged in some pursuit worthy of you. This is the subject which interests me most; for a long time it has been the object of all my thoughts." [63] And indeed in more than one passage he indicates his sense of how near and constant her sympathy and influence were. "I wish to say more, but in this way and at this moment cannot; and, besides, as I have never a good idea which does not occur to you first, it is deemed unnecessary." [64]

Whatever her influence was, it is certain that she followed every step of his career with passionate anxiety and interest. His doings, his plans, his projects—she demanded to be kept cognizant of them all. "As soon as you have formed any determinations, I conjure you to inform me of them as soon as possible. I know that entreaty is not necessary. I am too proud of your confidence to affect a doubt of it; but my mind is anxious, impatiently anxious in regard to your future destiny.

118

Where you are going, what will occupy you, how this will terminate, employ me continually; and, when, forgetful of myself, my brain is dizzy with a multitude of projects, my poor little heart cries out—and when shall we meet?" [65]

Naturally what interested and fired Theodosia most was her father's plan of Mexican domination and sovereignty. After the Hamilton duel, in 1804, had ruined his political prospects in the United States and he had parted forever with that phase of ambition in his farewell speech to the Senate as Vice-President, Burr traveled through the great Western country and conceived his cloudy scheme of empire. Details are vague in the narrative of historians, as they were probably vague in Burr's own mind. But that they included some dream sovereignty of some kind for himself and Theodosia and her boy, established on the ruins of Spanish-American dominion, is hardly to be questioned. Two brief but immensely significant passages alone are sufficient to prove this. There is the sentence already quoted in which Blennerhassett, writing to Alston, refers to "your *sovereign* in expectancy," [66] and the still more remarkable words of Theodosia, written after it was all over and referring to a possible disturbance in Mexico: "Thank God, I am not near my subjects; all my care and real tenderness

119

might be forgotten in the strife." [67]   The scheme, whatever it was, failed hopelessly, partly because it was in its nature too vast to be realized, still more, no doubt, because Burr was practically incapable of keeping up with the great sweep of his imagination.

What concerns us is Theodosia's attitude towards the whole affair.   First how did she herself feel? Were her imagination and her ambition excited? There is no evidence that in general she took much interest in politics.   It was persons, not causes, that primarily appealed to her.   Yet we must remember her mother's admiring comment on the triumph of the great Catherine, and there is also in Theodosia's own remark about her Mexican subjects something which suggests that the cloudy vision had taken a hold upon her fancy.   Sensitive and sensible as she was, there are touches implying that she was not wholly indifferent to the distinctions of the great world: "I would to Heaven I could be with you," she writes to her father in Paris.   "I long to visit a region where the Muses and Graces have some favorites . . . and circumstances have, for a long time, been inimical to my advancement in any respect." [68]

But, whatever her own personal aspirations, there can be no question about her passionate interest in her father's success. She would have liked to see him emperor of the world, and devoutly believed that he deserved to be so. As to Mexico, her grief at the abandonment of the project is intense and lingering and shows in reference after reference in her later letters: "No doubt there are many other roads to happiness, but this appeared so perfectly suitable to you, so complete a remuneration for all the past; it so entirely coincided with my wishes relative to you, that I cherished it as my comfort, even when illness scarcely allowed me any hope of witnessing its completion." [69]

And when the project was abandoned, when failure and disappointment came, her affection, her devotion, were unfailing and illimitable, as in all other phases of her father's career. She loved him when she was a child, she loved him in her mature age, loved him for his gentleness, for his thoughtfulness, for what seemed to her his unselfishness and consideration, and because he liked to see people happy. When misfortune completely overtook him and he was being tried in Richmond for his life, she stepped right out and stood beside him, as proud to be his daughter as when he was Vice-President of the United States. He had nothing to be ashamed of, nor had she, and why should not innocence turn the world's hatred into kindly cheerfulness? She writes of her stay in Richmond during his trial: "Indeed, my father, so far from accepting of sympathy, has continually animated all around him. . . . Since my residence here, of which some days and a night were passed in the penitentiary, our little family circle has been a scene of uninterrupted gayety." [70]

Far more astonishing than the child's devotion and loyalty is her inexhaustible belief. She was not only completely subjugated by her father's charm, "I find that your presence threw a lustre on everything around you. Everything is gayer, more elegant, more pleasant where you are," [71] she accepted him as perfect with an almost superhuman perfection: "Indeed, I witness your extraordinary fortitude with new wonder at every new misfortune. Often, after reflecting on this subject, you appear to me so superior, so elevated above all other men; I contemplate you with such a strange mixture of humility, admiration, reverence, love, and pride, that very little superstition would be necessary to make me worship you as a superior being; such enthusiasm does your character excite in me. . . . I had rather not live than not be the daughter of such a man." [72] And this was written after the conspiracy, after the trial, when Burr had certainly shown all the defects he had.

Perhaps, in spite of her enthusiasm, she was not quite oblivious of all of them. If you look very carefully, you can find an occasional touch of criticism. Errors? Oh yes, he makes errors, slight ones: "You know, I love to convict you of an error, as some philosophers seek for spots in the sun." [73] And, for all his superhumanity, even she suspects him of delaying and dallying too idly with the sweet of life: "I tell you this, because I begin to think that Hannibal has got to Capua." [74] Yet these are trifles, and the sun of her existence remained for the most part unspotted.

And then one thinks of the man as history sees him. To Americans in general to-day he is simply one branded with eternal ignominy and with the mark of Cain upon his forehead. In the most charitable view, it must be admitted that, while he may have liked to see people happy, he made many people wretched. He ran a wild, disordered career, with little spiritual guide except his own whim and the passionate fancy of the moment, with little real regard to whom or what he sacrificed. And if sexual morals have any social significance whatever, he was certainly an abominable reprobate. Worse still, as it would have appeared to him, and possibly to Theodosia, he was not only a bad man, he was a small man. By a petty love of mystery and disguise, by a constitutional incapacity for living with great purposes, he managed to give to even vast designs a perpetual flavor of comic opera. The little things of life were just as important to him as the big, and while such a disposition may not be fatal to happiness, it surely is to greatness. Yet this superb woman, with an intellect as keen as her character was lofty, made an idol of him.

And it must be admitted that a peculiar and exquisite tragic pathos is infused into her love and loyalty by the very worthlessness of the object, as so often happens in this troubled and unequal world. She had the nobler, the finer, the more dignified nature, as well as the stronger, and all her nobility and dignity were lavished upon Aaron Burr.

Yet with it all there was a certain similarity between them in their eternal childlikeness. With one of his charming touches of insight, Burr says: "Oh yes! I knew how much of a child you were when I sent the pretty things. Just such another child is *son père.*" [75] The world, to both of them, was instinctively a matter of pretty things. Love, hate, empire, life, were toys to be trifled with and flung away, in view of the vast ocean of illusion, which tosses up men and gods and worlds and hopes in ceaseless admired disorder forever and forever.

V

MRS. JAMES MADISON

CHRONOLOGY

Dorothea Payne (Todd) Madison.

Born, North Carolina, May 20, 1772.

Removed to Philadelphia, 1783.

Married John Todd, January 7, 1790.

Married James Madison, September 15, 1794.

Madison, Secretary of State, 1801-1809.

Madison, President, 1809-1817.

Retired to Montpelier, 1817.

Madison died, June 28, 1836.

Died, July 8, 1849.

MRS. JAMES MADISON

I

THERE are centripetal and centrifugal spirits, spirits which turn naturally within, however they may be forced without, which live interior lives, sometimes tormented and perturbed, sometimes sunny, tranquil, and serene, and spirits which shrink from themselves or forget themselves, finding their activity, if not their happiness, in the turmoil of the outward world. Assuredly Mrs. Madison's spirit was centrifugal, if any ever was. She loved life in all its whirl and movement. She had long, pleasant, even merry years of it. In the main outward good fortune waited upon her, with a varied if not always uninterrupted felicity, and she had in herself those rich resources of spiritual sunshine which give a golden tinge to even gray days and somber moments. A lady who had known her intimately for many years says of her when she was nearly sixty years old: "She certainly has always been and still is one of the happiest of human beings, . . . she seems to have no place

about her which could afford a lodgment for care
or trouble. Time seems to favor her as much as
fortune." [1] John Quincy Adams reports much the
same thing, in his dry, crusty fashion: "She is a
woman of placid, equable temperament, and less
susceptible of laceration by the scourges of the
world abroad than most others." [2] But the Shakespearean way of touching such a temperament, as
of touching anything, is the loveliest and most
satisfying:

"Happy is your grace,
That can translate the stubbornness of fortune
Into so quiet and so sweet a style."

Dorothea—or Dolly—Payne Madison's external
life was certainly varied and picturesque enough to
involve any sort of experience. Her parents were
well-to-do Virginians, but she was born, in 1772,
when they were visiting North Carolina. Her
father became affiliated with the Quakers and removed to Philadelphia when she was a girl. There
she was brought up in Quaker surroundings and
there, early in 1790, she married a young Quaker
named John Todd. She bore two children, of whom
the eldest, a boy, survived, and after a brief period
of married life, her husband perished in the yellow-
fever epidemic. In the autumn of 1794 she married
Madison and was swept into the whirl of his politi-

cal fortunes. For eight years she was the wife of the Secretary of State and practically the head of the national hospitality, since Jefferson was a widower. For another eight years she was the wife of the President. In 1817 she and her husband retired to Madison's estate, Montpelier, in Virginia, and they had no further connection with public life. But though retired, they were anything but solitary, and till her husband's death in 1836, and till her own in 1849, she was always the center of a crowding, hurrying, shifting pressure of human interest.

It is hardly fair to infer that the woman had no inner life because we hear nothing of it. But it is safe to assume that the rush of external impressions left her little time to brood upon her own soul, its nature or its workings. The brief records of conversation with her suggest little of inward experience; but they are brief. On the other hand, we have a considerable number of her letters and it must be confessed that they are distinctly external and trivial, the letters of a woman of the world, kindly, affectionate, tender, but not revealing much of spiritual activity and suggesting that there was not much to reveal. Occasionally she remarks that she is so shut up and has seen so few people that she has nothing to write.[3] Apparently it does not occur to her that the adventures of the soul may also have their interest.

She had the elements of the feminine education of that day, but little more, and she had never the time or the desire to educate herself in the field of books. Her letters give astonishingly little evidence of any familiarity with the thought of the world. In later years she does ask for a novel: "By the bye, do you ever get hold of a clever novel, new or old, that you could send me? I bought Cooper's last, but did not care for it, because the story was so full of horrors." [4] She even pushes her enthusiasm so far as to call for the "Romance of History." [5] But we do not hear that she got it or read it. Her knowledge of the human heart, which was probably extensive in its kind, was not obtained from books.

Nor did her Quaker training give her much in the way of accomplishments or prepare her for æsthetic enjoyment. The house at Montpelier was full of busts, paintings, and drawings, some of them by artists of high quality. She showed these things to her guests. Perhaps she enjoyed them herself. The only allusion to music is somewhat mechanical: "The music-box is playing beside me, and seems well adapted to solitude." [6] Montpelier was situated in a beautiful region and the natural beauty was heightened by art. She must have felt all this, but

MRS. JAMES MADISON

she does not speak of it. It is said that she was an
ardent gardener and tended her flowers with much
devotion. We have a charming picture of her, ris-
ing very early, while her visitors were asleep, and
working in her long apron among the dewy blos-
soms.[7] She plucked them and then bestowed them
lavishly upon her friends. For her existence seems
to have been mainly one of give, give, give, give
time, give goods, give life. As was said of another
lady, of equally abundant temper, "she was too
generous with herself." And giving is no doubt an
excellent and charming thing. Only perhaps those
give best who also sometimes take, at least a little.

Thus, if religion consists in charity and external
kindliness, it is evident that Mrs. Madison was
rich in it, and certainly this is the part of religion
that is most serviceable. Again, I should not undertake to deny that she had depths of spiritual experience. But there are no signs of it, and the
signs are mainly the other way. In talk with
Ticknor she defended the Quakers, as she would
have defended any friend.[8] In mature years she
was a faithful attendant upon the Episcopal service. But she had comparatively little suffering or
depression to drive her to God, and she lived curiously remote in spirit from the evil of the world.
When she hears of the burning of Mount Vernon,

she exclaims against "the wickedness of men and women." [9] But somehow it does not seem to touch her very directly. What is most noticeable about her spiritual attitude is a large and sweet tolerance, which she may have imbibed in part from her Quaker connections, but which I think was also largely owing to her husband and to her great friend, Thomas Jefferson. This open and sunny charity is by no means the worst of religions, though perhaps even Jefferson would have been hardly ready to accept Anatole France's charming formulation of it: "Tolerance is so dear to me that I would sacrifice for it even the sweetest of beliefs."

II

And so Mrs. Madison's life is to be studied chiefly in her relations to other human beings, and we may begin with the nearest, her husband, or husbands. As to the first, John Todd, we know less than we could wish, and we are not even quite clear as to Dolly's feeling about him. It is said that she was averse to the marriage and only yielded to pressure from her father; but such stories count for little. In any case, there is sufficient evidence of later affection and Todd appears to have been a sober, manly, hard-working, devoted fellow who would have made her happy if he had lived. Her circumstances after his death are again somewhat doubtful; but for a time she lived with her mother, who, in Dolly's delicate phrase, "after my father's death received into her house some gentlemen as boarders." [10] Among these boarders was Aaron Burr, and it would seem as if a beautiful young widow might have been a tempting morsel for Burr's universal rapacity. Nothing of the sort appears, however, and instead, Madison selected Burr as the means of getting himself introduced to the lady who had attracted his attention. We have the brief note in which Dolly announced the event: "Dear friend, thou must come to me. Aaron Burr says that the 'great little Madison' has asked to be brought to see me this evening." [11] He came, and the courtship progressed rapidly.

In Mrs. Todd's acceptance of this new suitor there was probably a complication of motives. He was twenty years older than she. He had previously made unsuccessful attempts at marriage, the lady in one case having lightly tossed him aside for a showy young parson. Though Madison's face was distinguished and even handsome, he was far from imposing in appearance, and in later life Irving said of him, "Poor Jemmy! he is but a withered little apple-john." [12] On the other hand, he was already prominent politically and seemed destined to be more so, and there was a rather remarkable similarity of temperament between the two. Dolly may not have conceived a romantic passion for him, but she cherished a warm, sincere affection which lasted all his life.

And Madison thoroughly deserved it. He played a great part in his country's history, and on the whole played it adequately. It must be understood at the start that he was essentially an intellectualist, a thinker rather than a doer. From his youth he read widely, and thought widely also, if not always very deeply. The critical value of this broad and temperate study in the building of the national Constitution was immense, and Madison's sober and solidly reasoned judgment most ably balanced and sustained the ardent enthusiasm of Hamilton. When it came to executive government later, the intellectualist was somewhat less successful, and the ill-managed War of 1812 did not help his reputation, while his naturally impartial and judicial temper became more or less involved in the party passions of the time. Still, even in this regard he was much more moderate than Jefferson, and in the main he will always stand in history as a wise, discreet, and luminous spirit. I like, as coming from that source, his wife's summary of his qualities in her letter to Jackson after her husband's death: "He, who had never lost sight of that consistency, symmetry, and beauty of character in all its parts, which rendered his own transcendent as a whole and worthy of the best aspirations." [13]

This summary, however, omits the charming humor which rendered Madison delightful in private intercourse. In public he was formal and conventional enough; but with his intimates he had a graceful gayety which seems rarely to have failed. Indeed, it clung to him to the very last. In his fatal illness a friend begged him not to try to talk in his enforced recumbent position. He answered, summing up the career of the statesman and diplomat, "Oh, I always talk most easily when I lie." [14] And his credibly reported dying words have a grace and significance which seldom appear in such a situation. On the morning of his death his niece gave him his breakfast and, observing that he had difficulty in swallowing, asked, "What is the matter, Uncle Jeames?" "Nothing more than a change of mind, my dear." [15] Shortly after he was dead.

It is generally supposed that Mrs. Madison was not closely involved in her husband's political interests. This is probably true. At the same time, there are bits in her letters which seem to indicate that she followed the general currents of the time with intelligent attention, and her husband's letters to her also show that he confided in her and trusted her. I relish particularly the mixture of public and intimately feminine concern which appears in the following passage referring to the movement of ships of war: "No *Constitution* heard of yet; the *Hornet* went to take despatches and to let them know our determination to fight for our rights. I wrote by the *Hornet* to Mrs. Barlow and begged her to send me anything she thought suitable in the way of millinery." [16] But in another letter she writes to Madison himself with a simplicity, sweetness, and dignity which would be becoming to any wife in any age: "You know I am not much of a politician, but I am extremely anxious to hear (as far as you think proper) what is going forward in the Cabinet. On this subject I believe you would not desire your wife to be the active partisan that our neighbor is, Mrs. L., nor will there be the slightest danger, while she is conscious of her want of talents, and the diffidence in expressing those opinions, always imperfectly understood by her sex." [17]

It is again a query how far the wife shared and stimulated her husband's political ambition. That she liked and appreciated his high standing and office is evident enough. What woman would not? But it seems quite clear that she early made up her mind that her part in the matter was social. She would see to it that the Madisons were generally known and well beloved, that the rancor of party was softened as much as possible in social relations, and most admirably and successfully did she labor to that end.

Nor is there any direct proof that she often endeavored to exert her influence for political purposes. If she put her friends into office, we do not hear of it. In 1806 and 1807 there was a rather sharp rivalry between Madison and Monroe for the presidential succession and Mrs. Madison is said to have spoken bitterly about Monroe.[18] Also, at that period, John Randolph, who was for the moment a Monroe partisan, writes to his candidate of his rival, as follows: "There is another consideration which I know not how to touch. You, my dear sir, cannot be ignorant—although of all mankind you, perhaps, have the least cause to know it—how deeply the respectability of any character may be impaired by an unfortunate matrimonial connection—I can pursue this subject no further."[19] What Randolph meant he does not explain, nor can anyone else. On the other hand, Blaine, writing at a later period, says: "Mrs. Madison saved the administration of her husband, held him back from the extremes of Jeffersonism, and enabled him to

escape from the terrible dilemma of the War of
'12. But for her, De Witt Clinton would have been
chosen President in 1812." [20] Perhaps it would be
as difficult to substantiate this claim as to support
the insinuations of Randolph. But it is probable
that the wife's broad, kindly, and tolerant temper,
so akin to his own, sustained and strengthened the
husband in a habitual attitude of lenience and
generosity.

Mrs. Madison's most intense and direct contact
with politics undoubtedly came during the trying
years of the war. She may not have taken great
interest in the more abstract aspects of the matter;
but there were personal features that could not but
come home to her. There were too brief moments
of triumph, chiefly in connection with the brilliant
naval operations. One bit of anecdote focuses
the twinkling gleams of glory in an effective manner. A great ball was given in Washington, to
celebrate the captures of the *Alert* and the *Guerrière*. In the midst of all the gayety Lieutenant
Paul Hamilton arrived with the news of the taking
of the *Macedonian* and bearing her flag. He was
ushered into the hall with shouts of joy and con-
gratulation, and presented the flag to Mrs. Madison before it was hung on the wall with those of
the other captured vessels.[21]

One likes to afford her at least this fleeting instant of enjoyment, for the remainder of the war
period was largely a time of anxiety and annoyance. The culmination came in the British seizure
of the capital. Such a disaster was hardly looked
for, even up to the last moment. Mrs. Madison
sat in the White House, waiting for the return
of her husband and the Cabinet, who had gone out
to see the fighting. Dinner was on the table,[22] and
every one expected a safe, if not a triumphant
result. Then a messenger came hurrying in with
word that the British were advancing and the White
House must be abandoned in the utmost haste.
Mrs. Madison gathered up what she could and
went. The story that she herself cut the portrait
of Washington from the frame will probably never
be quite disposed of, though she could not have
done it, as the picture could be reached only by a
ladder and was removed under her directions by
the servants.[23] But she took the valuables that
seemed to her most essential and hurried in her
carriage across the Potomac, seeking refuge with
friends, while her home and her possessions were
destroyed almost before her eyes. In a short time
it was all over, the British had retired, and she was
able to go back. But the shock and strain of it

must have been severe, and such agonizing memories made peace doubly welcome, when at last it came.

Through all these agitations, and through all the varied experiences of a long career, it is evident that Madison clung to his wife with constant and untroubled affection. He was a man who, for all his public activity, loved home and domestic tenderness, and he appreciated them where he found them. And the wife's affection for her husband is equally undisputed. They had no children, and though they both were fondly attached to the son by her first marriage, they both felt that they had little in the world besides each other. High-wrought romantic ardor was hardly in Dolly's nature; but perhaps she was all the more capable of a gentle glow of persistent devotion. When she is obliged by illness and the need of treatment to leave her husband's side, she longs for him. She is unable to sleep from anxiety about him, she says, and she emphasizes the grief "I feel at even so short a separation from one who is all in all to me." [24] When she is well and with him, without relatives and friends to distract her, she writes, "You may imagine me the very shadow of my husband." [25] In later years, during his long illness, she is most faithful in attendance, and for months she remains near at hand, ready to minister to all his wants. After his death she clings to the tradition of his glory, and I like especially her desperate determination to save his papers when they were threatened by fire. It is true that the papers represented a substantial money value when she sorely needed it, but they represented far more than money, the memory of past glory and delight. How vivid is the picture of her, suddenly awakened from sound sleep, with the smoke swirling about her, but refusing to be saved till the servants had gathered together the precious papers, and then, when the fire was extinguished, "laughingly returning, clad in a black velvet gown and nightcap, with bare feet." [26]

III

This episode, together with her conduct during the British invasion and in many other instances, proves that Mrs. Madison was no weakling, given over to merely external diversions, however she may have liked the flutter and turmoil of the outer world. She was perfectly capable of a firm and quiet self-possession and she had a solid, though dignified, gift for managing herself and others. She swayed her household skillfully and successfully for many years, and seems to have had all the qualities necessary to do so. Her health was not at all times perfect, and when illness overcame her she fell

141

very briefly into a tone of discouragement. But in the main she had ample vigor, which lasted into advanced life, as is shown in the pretty story of her athletic accomplishments when she was sixty. "One time on the portico, she took Anna by the hand, saying: 'Come, let us run a race. I do not believe you can outrun me. Madison and I often run races here when the weather does not allow us to walk.' And she really did run very briskly." [27] The picture of the fourth ex-President of the United States and his wife running rainy-day races when they were approaching three and four score has a peculiar gayety.

To have carried on such a vast establishment as hers at all obviously required a good deal of executive experience. Madison himself had a natural instinct of order and system; but he left the domestic management mainly to her, and she was altogether adequate to it. A contemporary writer says: "Everything that came beneath her immediate and personal sway, the care and entertainment of visitors, the government of servants, the whole policy of the interior, was admirably managed with equal grace and efficacy." [28]

I should like a little more light on the question of servants. These were, of course, all, or almost all, slaves, and there seems to have been the horde

142

of them usual in large Virginian establishments at that time. Miss Martineau gives a striking account of the luxury of service in the Madison household: "During all our conversations one or another slave was perpetually coming to Mrs. Madison for the great bunch of keys; two or three more lounged about in the house, leaning against the door posts or the corner of the sofa; and the attendance of others was no less indefatigable in my own apartment." [29] The colored man, Jennings, who lived long in the family, both slave and free, declares that Madison himself was always lenient and gentle, would never strike a slave or allow any one else to do so,[30] and it is said that the servants turned rather to him than to his wife.[31] But this was natural enough, since the domestic discipline must have rested chiefly with her. Her own maid, when told by Mrs. Smith that she had a good mistress, answered with the greatest warmth: "Yes, the best, I believe, in the world. I am sure I would not change her for any mistress in the whole country." [32]

The crucial question in all these domestic matters is money, and here it cannot be said that Mrs. Madison distinguished herself quite so much as in some other aspects. It is notable that the three great Virginian Presidents who followed Washington and Adams were all unfortunate in money matters, all lived with a rather unwarrantable profusion, and all died poor or left embarrassed estates. Madison himself was not inclined to personal extravagance. Jennings even tells us that his master "never had but one suit at a time. He had some poor relatives that he had to help, and wished to set them an example of economy in the matter of dress." [33] But both he and his wife were accustomed to Virginian hospitality, and their position in Washington and at Montpelier almost necessitated vast and constant entertaining, which could not be carried on without expense. They had numbers of guests at table, and the table was always bountifully supplied. Critics from abroad even suggested that the display in this regard approached the vulgar; but Mrs. Madison laughed and said that Europeans might consider that scarcity was elegance, but that the exhaustless wealth of our country was best shown in liberal entertainment.[34] Yet it all cost money. The wines at least had to be imported from niggard Europe, and niggard Europe charged a round price for them. Then if you had guests, you had to have furniture. The White House was large, and the house at Montpelier far from small, and the rooms had to be made and kept habitable, and it could not be done for nothing. Also, to come and go everywhere, you had to have conveyances.

Coaches did not cost like limousines, but they cost enough, more than it was always convenient for a hard-pressed Virginia planter to pay.

And there was giving as well as spending— giving to relatives, giving to friends, giving to the world at large. Mrs. Madison was interested in various charities; she was ready and anxious to extend her kindness to all who came within reach of it. It is said that during the war, whenever soldiers marched by, "she always sent out and invited them in to take wine and refreshments, giving them liberally of the best in the house." [35] Such cordial acts are charming, but they do have their effect on the bills.

Consequently Madison, even in his more flourishing period, was more or less embarrassed. There was money to be had, but it did not always come easily or at once. "He lived like a rich man," says his biographer, "but his payments were not always made promptly. Mr. Voss had occasionally to remind him that his rent was overdue, and sometimes a creditor politely dunned him; but a number of friends owed money to him, and he was never charged with avoiding his pecuniary obligations." [36] While it is said that his wife was a good financial manager—and she probably was—it is not likely that she was a great force for thrift.

145

After her husband's death the situation was by no means improved. In fact, the pressure was so great that, if the stories are to be believed, she was reduced to absolute need. Jennings says that she "sometimes suffered for the necessaries of life. While I was a servant to Mr. Webster, he often sent me to her with a market-basket full of provisions, and told me whenever I saw anything in the house that I thought she was in need of to take it to her. I often did this and occasionally gave her small sums from my own pocket." [37] It would take a sunny disposition indeed to endure this sort of thing patiently; but it did not last, as Congress relieved the distress of the ex-President's widow by purchasing his papers and putting the money paid into trust for her benefit.

It must at least be remembered, however, that Mrs. Madison's fault was not self-indulgence, and that, if she ruined herself, it was largely for the sake of those she loved. She was devoted to her relatives. Her younger sister lived with her almost as a daughter, and the letters written to her after her marriage are full of penetrating tenderness: "Anna, I'm dying to come to your country. If I could only be with you, how glad I should be." [38] She was equally attached to her nieces and turned to them in later years with a clinging affection. It is said that at first the Madisons felt that her own family predominated among her guests and that she was inclined to make more of her relatives than of his.[39] But she soon disposed of this criticism and proved that she had quite tenderness enough for all. One of the most charming things about her is her devotion to Madison's mother, who lived on at Montpelier to the age of ninety-seven. In speaking of her daughter-in-law's care and solicitude, the old lady said to a friend: "In other respects I am feeble and helpless, and owe everything to her: she is my mother now." [40]

The greatest burden on Mrs. Madison's purse and on her thoughts was undoubtedly the son of her first marriage, Payne Todd. Payne seems to have been a handsome and attractive boy, and his stepfather was almost as fond of him as his mother was. But he received more fondness than discipline. His education was erratic, and the great position of his parents gave him social advantages and social temptations which he was but ill-fitted to resist. His temper was rather easy and self-indulgent than vicious; but the results were much the same. He drank, he spent, he gambled, and then the father and mother were called upon to pay his debts. His mother's letters, as printed, have no bitterness, and if there is reproach in them, it is so gentle that it

147

merely emphasizes her affection. "Everyone inquires after you; but, my dear son, it seems to be
the wonder of them all that you should stay away
from us for so long a time. And now I am ashamed
to tell, when asked, how long my only child has
been absent from the home of his mother." [41]   To
the criticism of friends and enemies she had but the
one mother's answer: "My poor boy! Forgive his
eccentricities, for his heart is right." [42]   To her the
heart was all. And maternal pity and anxiety seem
to be the last emotions that hovered about her in
this world, for as she was dying, she was heard
to murmur repeatedly, "My poor boy!" [43]   Yet even
this constant trial could not essentially sour her or
shadow the sweetness of her spirit. That serenity
and good humor, which her friend Jefferson esteemed the most valuable of all human gifts and
qualities [44] and which perhaps in the beginning
spoiled her son, made her suffer less than some
might have suffered over the results of the spoiling.

IV

Moreover, from this misery, as from others, she
sought refuge in the amusing tumult of the world.
The analysis of the social motive, the impulse which
drives men and women into the crowding bustle of
their fellows, as against the peaceful attractions

of their own firesides, is curious though perhaps not altogether profitable. There is first, and, as we like to think, foremost, the element of kindliness, of real human sympathy and kinship with other human hearts, and this is usually present in some degree, and cannot be wholly discounted. But there are other elements less amiable, in most cases, if not in all, and it is doubtful whether simple human fellow‑ship would drive many of us over our thresholds quite so often as we go. There is the element of pure curiosity. We are always impelled to saturate the emptiness of our own lives with the petty details of the lives of others. What gown did Mrs. Jones wear? Did she really dismiss her cook? What did her husband say when he found unexpected guests at dinner? These are minor matters, but they ruffle the surface of existence and prevent us from seeing too far into the murky depths. Then there are the varying forms of subtle egotism to take us out into the world. There is the altruistic motive. We want to be of use, to do something, to help somebody. The deepest impulse of the ego to project itself perhaps shows in the cry, "I want the world to be better for my having lived in it." Or there is the simple pleasure of self-assertion, without any altruistic excuse whatever. We have gifts and powers and charms and attractions; we think we have, we hope we have. If we have, why not display them, why not indulge in the delight of having others tell us so? Their assurance, even though we suspect it to be somewhat false and flattering, is a great support to our own. Finally, perhaps the strongest of all social motives is the sheer desire to escape from ourselves. Even when our own society has charm, it is possible to be surfeited with it. And for most of us solitude is crowded with thoughts and vain desires and long regrets, from which almost any escape is often welcome. Only, there are people so fortunately constituted that when they go among others they instantly forget themselves, flow out instinctively into the movement and the life that are going on about them. There are others who carry self with them wherever they go, and who find the monster more intrusive, the greater the bustle and hurry in which they live; to such, self is the greatest of social obstacles, and, go where they will, they cannot escape it.

Whatever the motive for social activity, there can be no question as to the force of habit in regard to it. There is the habit of going, and the habit of home. Go, and you will wish to go. Stay, and going will in the end become irksome and distasteful. A week's trial will establish this truth for anyone. When you have passed a peaceful week at home with work and books, you wonder why you ever stir out. As the author of the *Imitation* expresses it, in his crystal language, which even a high-school freshman can understand yet the greatest scholar cannot render with all its clinging savor: "Cella continuata dulcescit; et male custodita tædium generat."

And it is certain that Mrs. Madison had the habit of going. No doubt she had quite sufficient dignity and self-control to accept solitude when circumstances imposed it upon her. But her natural bent was centrifugal, to turn always outward to the swift commerce of the world. This bent, I think, was almost too strong for her to form and maintain intimate friendships; she was too generally expansive for them. It may be that married women rarely have such friendships, anyway, except as they hold over from premarital youth. The shadow of a husband, always likely to overhear the most intimate confidences, naturally affects such confidences with a sort of chilling reserve. At any rate, I see no sign of close friendships in Mrs. Madison's case, and we have no letters of personal outpouring to anyone but her own family, if even with them it may be called such. Yet it is clear that she had the qualities that make for friendship, directness, sincerity, cordiality. When Mrs. Smith visits her, the

151

visitor is taken at once into the inmost family life.
"No restraint, no ceremony. Hospitality is the presiding genius of this house, and Mrs. Madison is kindness personified." [45] She was willing to give herself, if you could take it; but it had to be snatched in passing, for always it was on the way somewhere else.

And she did enjoy a crowd, liked to live in the tide, in the flood, to have people coming and going about her perpetually: "You know, I usually like the routs all too well." [46] There was once a lady who said, as did Charles Lamb, that she should be glad to meet and talk for a few minutes with everybody in the world, and the same lady declared that she never saw a visitor coming to her door without being pleased, a statement which might provoke some cynical persons to the assertion of the exact opposite. But clearly Mrs. Madison had precisely the temper of that lady. When she was in Washington, either entertaining for Jefferson or as mistress of the White House, it might be expected that she would be the center of ever-shifting throngs, and of course she was. Guests of all sorts crowded about her, and she had a word and a smile and a heart for all of them. But when she retired into the country, it was very much the same. It is true that Montpelier was by natural environment a solitary place. But the genius of Mrs. Madison constantly contrived to fill it. There were swarms of relatives, there were swarms of Virginians, there were swarms of her husband's political associates, with not a few of differing opinions mixed in; and no stranger of importance came from Europe without visiting both Monticello and Montpelier. A few more or less could make no possible difference. When Mrs. Smith arrived, the hostess asked why she did not bring her little girls. Mrs. Smith had feared they might be troublesome. But the lady laughed: "I should not have known they were here among all the rest, for at this moment we have only three and twenty in the house." "Three and twenty!" cried Mrs. Smith. "And where do you store them?"

"Oh, we have house room in plenty."[47] And where house room failed, heart room made up for it. Ninety to dine "at one table—put up on the lawn under a thick arbor,"[48] was a casual occurrence. Even after her husband's death, it was much the same: she was still the center of a throng of people, people of all sorts who observed her curiously and were observed by her and made life twinkle and sparkle up to the very verge of the grave.

After this elaborate development of the Book of Numbers, it is hardly necessary to say that she was a social success. In her youth she seems to have been very beautiful. People stopped to look at her in the street and a friend remonstrated with her, laughingly, "Really, Dolly, thou must hide thy face, there are so many staring at thee." [49] And the beauty appears to have been of a lasting sort, a matter of grace and charm which endure through the changing years. She understood the art of dress. Sometimes she clung to early Quaker simplicity, and again she sought the aid of all the fashions, appearing in silks and satins, feathers and the turbans which seem so odd to us at present. Also, there were what would appear to some of us drawbacks to her charm. She used paint and powder with a freedom and constancy which her great-granddaughters might envy — used them skillfully and without excess, say some; but there was a grim Federalist parson who visited her and declared with rude vigor: "Mrs. Madison, though originally of a Quaker family, was dressed very splendidly, with a crown on her head. Her face and neck were obviously daubed with paint so as fairly to glisten." [50] Also, she had the even more deplorable habit of using snuff. Theodosia Burr visited her in 1803 and says, "She is still pretty; but, oh, the unfortunate propensity to snuff-taking." [51] And there is the homely anecdote in connection with Henry Clay, not uncharacteristic, though perhaps not of the surest authenticity. Mrs. Madison offered Clay a pinch, which he accepted in his usual dignified manner. Then she "put her hand into her pocket and pulling out a bandanna handkerchief, said, 'Mr. Clay, this is for rough work,' at the same time applying it in the proper place, 'and this,' producing a fine lace handkerchief from another pocket, 'is my polisher.' She suited the action to the words, removing from her nose the remaining grains of snuff." [52] Truly, other times, other manners.

Yet these things do not seem to have greatly diminished the lady's attraction, and one of the most delightful stories about her is the remark of an admirer, who was defending her against the charge of vanity. "But you tell me she used rouge and powder." "Yes, yes," said the admirer, "she did; but it was to please and gratify those who were thrown with her, not because she was fond of admiration." [53] Which recalls the character in the French comedy who was accused of vanity because he looked constantly in the glass: "It is not vanity, but simply because it gives me such pleasure to look at myself."

And apparently her popularity was almost universal, as universal as popularity can ever be in this critical world. I have searched quite widely for fault-finding, but discover astonishingly little. Now and then a note of dissonance does occur. Her friend, Mrs. Smith, after a paragraph of ecstatic praise, makes this comment, which I do not in the least understand: "Ah, why does she not in all things act with the same propriety? She would be too much beloved if she added all the virtues to all the graces." [54] Seward, who was inclined to be censorious, protests against her social prominence in later years: "All the world paid homage to her, saying that she was dignified and attractive. It is the fashion to say so. But, I confess, I thought more true dignity would have been displayed by her remaining, in her widowhood, in the ancient country mansion of her illustrious husband." [55] And again: "I had little opportunity, however, to judge of Mrs. Madison. But her dress, conversation, air, and everything showed me that she was a woman to whom fashion was necessary in her old age." [56] Yet this querulousness is rare. The general tone of admiration and affection among her friends appears in the words of Mrs. Smith: "It seems to me that such manners would disarm envy itself, and conciliate even enemies"; [57] and the colored man, Jennings, gives the same testimony as to inferiors, "She was beloved by everybody in Washington, white and colored." [58]

And she enjoyed the popularity, and why should she not? Her husband was sometimes bored and wearied with it. At the first inauguration ball, in 1809, he confided to Mrs. Smith, "I would much rather be in bed." [59] After the same grand occasion, which might probably be regarded as the acme of American social entertainment, Mrs. Smith herself, a young and eager woman, notes, "Never do I recollect one night retiring with such a vacuum, such a dissatisfied craving, such a restlessness of spirit, such undefined, vague desires, as I do now." [60] But we get nothing of this sort from Mrs. Madison. The rush of people was the breath of life to her, and the emptiness came when she was cut off from it. When she is ill, she does murmur a little, "We have had a continual round of company, which has been burdensome." [61] But even in illness people help rather than hinder. And, to be sure, in such a vast human contact there were bound to be disagreeable incidents. There was the evening when President Jefferson insisted on throwing over etiquette and giving her precedence of the wife of the British minister, which caused a storm, as Mrs. Madison foresaw it would. Again, when she fled from her burning home and tried to take refuge with a former acquaintance, all the welcome she got was: "Mis' Madison! if that's you, come down and go out! Your husband has got mine out fighting, and, damn you, you shan't stay in my house; so get out." [62]

But these jarring notes were few and rare, since she had in such an eminent degree the social qualities which subdue or avert them. One such quality, indeed, seems not to have been present to any great degree: she was not a brilliant or witty talker. The best that a keen observer like Ticknor can find to say of her in this line is, "Her conversation was somewhat formal, but on the whole appropriate to her position and now and then amusing." [63] Yet clever talking, like Madame de Staël's or Madame Du Deffand's, often hurts rather than helps. Mrs. Madison knew how to ask kindly questions, and to smooth asperities. She hated argument and gently got rid of it: "I would rather fight with my hands than my tongue." [64] As to the latter member, she early devoted herself to the most important of lessons: "I am learning to hold my tongue well." [65]

In other words, she was by nature and by vast experience a mistress of the exquisite art of social tact, knew how to adapt herself to people and how to adapt people to each other. She entered into the lives of others, into the hearts of others, knowing that what went on there was very much what went on in her own, and using the knowledge for the increased comfort and happiness of everybody. I relish one little anecdote which shows how such a social being will instinctively follow Sarah Ripley's admirable principle that the law of love is higher than the law of truth. In her old age, when it was difficult for her to write, Mrs. Madison taught her niece to imitate her own writing so that friends might feel that they were getting letters directly from herself.[66] But by far the best and noblest testimony to Mrs. Madison's social tact is the remark of her niece in regard to her, "I always thought better of *myself* when I had been with Aunt Dolly." [67] How many people there are of whom the reverse is true. And can there be a higher triumph of social achievement?

One of the most notable concrete elements in Mrs. Madison's social tact was her remarkable memory. It is said that, with all her vast acquaintance, she rarely forgot a face or a name: "Possessing a most retentive memory, she never miscalled a name, or forgot the slightest incident connected with the personal history of anyone, and therefore impressed each individual with an idea of their importance in her esteem." [68] She would probably have agreed with General Lee, who possessed a similar gift, that it was no special mental endowment, but simply a matter of courteous attention to everybody, thus confirming the theory of Lord Chesterfield, that a discreet, quick, constant attention is the first and most important of social principles.

However this may be, it is interesting to think what a vast personal storehouse the woman's memory must have been, how thronged with faces of all sorts, faces quick, gay, delightful, no doubt sometimes distorted or hideous, but always interesting. And the memory clung by her to the end, and the people clung by her to the end. As Philip Hone recorded in his *Journal*, in 1842, "She is a *young* lady of fourscore [threescore and ten] years and upward, goes to parties and receives company, like the 'Queen of this new world.' " [69] And finding her own life thus in the busy life that was whirling all about her, she was able to keep up to the end that impression of felicity—felicity of circumstances, and still more of temperament, which is always associated with her. Yet her final comment, on leaving this earth, on which she had lived so widely, was, "My dear, do not trouble about it; there is nothing in *this* world worth really caring for." [70] And I should like to know whether it is true that she emphasized *this;* but in any case there are not many men or women who have been in a better position for making such a statement.

VI

MRS. JEFFERSON DAVIS

CHRONOLOGY

Varina Howell Davis.
Born, Natchez, Mississippi, May 7, 1826.
Married Jefferson Davis, February 26, 1845.
Davis President of the Confederacy, 1861-1865.
Son Joe killed by fall from window, 1864.
In England, 1867-1870.
Son Willie died, 1874.
Son Jeff died, 1878.
Davis died, December 6, 1889.
Daughter Winnie died, 1898.
In later years lived in New York.
Died, New York, October 16, 1906.

MRS. JEFFERSON DAVIS

I

WHICH was the greater tragedy, that of Mrs. Lincoln, who saw her husband murdered in the very hour of supreme triumph and culminating glory and was herself cast into darkness and despair, or that of Mrs. Davis, who saw her husband's heroic struggle, in which she so ardently shared, end in disaster and utter ruin? It is hard to say. And neither woman was peculiarly fitted to bear adversity in a chastened or humble spirit. In fact, there were a number of elements of resemblance between them. Also, they had the same colored seamstress, who gossiped about them both, though the gossip in Mrs. Davis's case is much less extensive.

Varina Howell Davis was born in Natchez in 1826. It is curiously significant of the tangle of relations connected with the Civil War that the wife of the President of the Southern Confederacy had Northern and Whig antecedents, while the wife of the President of the Union came distinctly from

163

the South. Miss Howell grew up in comfortable Southern surroundings and was well educated. In 1845 she married Jefferson Davis, then a widower without children and seventeen years older than she. She was closely associated with his brilliant career, as soldier and statesman, played a striking part in Washington society in the 'fifties, shared her husband's triumphs and disappointments during the four years' existence of the Confederacy, and saw all her hopes wiped out by the surrender of Lee. She was with her husband when he was captured, made desperate efforts to secure his release from prison, and was the intimate partner of his later wandering efforts and sorrows. After his death in 1889, she wrote an elaborate history of his career, and lived on somehow till 1906, having survived all of her six children but one daughter. She was always treated with respect in the South, as embodying great memories and departed glory; but her real life came to an end with that of the President of the Confederacy.

Mrs. Davis was not only well educated by good schooling in Philadelphia and by tutoring at home, but she profited by her education and continued it all her life. She read quite extensively. When she was sixteen, she "was reading hard to finish my course of English and Latin classics," [1] and she

164

quotes Latin in later years in a rather unusual fashion. She was able to talk intelligently with the
many men of distinction and power whom she en-
countered in her varied life—with statesmen, with
men of letters, even with men of science like Joseph
Henry. She kept up a close intellectual compan-
ionship with her husband, and he was a man of surprisingly active and well-stored mind. She aided
him greatly in much of his writing, and her *Life* of
him affords ample evidence that she had exceptional
gifts, both as a thinker and as a mistress of English
style. How much assistance, if any, she may have
had in the composition of the book, I do not know;
but the general tone of it must have been hers, and
it does her credit. The narrative instinct is as
marked in the picturesque account of Black Hawk's
career as the dramatic sense which emphasized the
effective, if somewhat dubious, incident of Lincoln's first taking the oath of allegiance to his
country before Jefferson Davis.[2]

Mrs. Davis's intelligence was not only active
and far-reaching, it was singularly acute and penetrating. Her observations on men and things are
always suggestive, even if one does not agree with
them. During her life in Washington she met the
most prominent statesmen of the middle of the century—Webster, Clay, Calhoun, Seward, and Sum-

ner—and her relations with the notable figures of
the Confederacy were even more intimate. She
analyzed all these distinguished personages with
constant and appreciative attention. Take, for example, this just and striking portrayal of one side
of the character of Judah P. Benjamin: "Mr.
Benjamin's courtesy in argument was like the
salute of the duellist to his antagonist whom he
intends to kill, if possible. He was master of the
art of inductive reasoning, and when he had smil-
ingly established his point, he dealt the *coup de
grâce* with a fierce joy which his antagonist fully
appreciated and resented. I never knew him in
those days to be very much in earnest without
infuriating his antagonist beyond measure." [3]

And Mrs. Davis seems to have been as intelligent
concretely as abstractly. She was a good housekeeper, could manage either her large city establishment in Richmond or the plantation of Brier-
field. She knew how work should be done, and
could do it herself, if necessary. Her enemies, who
found fault with everything, even asserted as proof
of her unaristocratic origin that she had done house-
work in her youth, rather a disgrace in a slave-
holding community. [4] But I like particularly her
pleasant picture of herself and her husband, in one
of the too rare tranquil eddies of their turbulent

MRS. JEFFERSON DAVIS

career, striving together to improve the old estate and toiling side by side in the garden, like Adam and Eve, then for recreation mounting their horses and riding whirlwind races, in which, according to her own account, the man hardly outspeeded the woman.[5] Or, in vivid contrast to this idyllic atmosphere, there is the crowding pressure of the wife's, the friend's, the housekeeper's interests in the pattering questions of a letter written in a moment of thrilling crisis: "Has Ives turned up? Did Johnston leave his family? Had Mrs. McLean got off? Did Mr. Minnegerode come out? Did we bring off anything when you came? Did you send the pest out of the way? Did you bring the brandy? Where is Joe?"[6]

Money is the supreme test of domestic management. Here again the critics are busy and murmur about Mrs. Davis's extravagance. No doubt she liked to spend and in a sense she was obliged to spend. At any rate, I find no evidence whatever of her being burdened with the load of debt that afflicted Mrs. Lincoln. There is a certain ungraciousness in her effort to protect herself during the last bitter days in Richmond, by storing up flour, which her husband strictly forbade her to carry away, in view of the privation and starvation about her.[7] But something must be forgiven to a mother

with little children. And after the war she had
to meet money difficulties which must have been
distressing and humiliating enough to one who
had been situated as she had. Thus, she writes
from England, in 1868: "We are too poor to
travel, so that I have seen nothing here except Liv-
erpool, and this little suburb yclept Waterloo. . . .
I never saw such an expensive country in my life.
It costs so much to dress even decently that I have
decided not to try, and I never accept any invita-
tions or go anywhere to dinner or elsewhere, not
even to an exhibition, except such as are free, for I
feel hourly the necessity of pinching at every
turn." [8]

As to Mrs. Davis's relations with her servants,
so significant in the slave-holding South, we have
little reliable testimony besides her own, which is
not unnaturally very favorable. She gives a beatific
picture of plantation life, of the sympathetic care
of master and mistress and the devotion of depend-
ents. In the main I have no doubt the picture is a
faithful likeness. Welles gives a rather hideous
story of a slave whom Mrs. Davis had personally
maltreated. [9] But similar improbable stories were
told even of General Lee. Mrs. Davis had a quick
and vigorous temper, which may possibly at times
have extended to her fingers as well as to her

tongue. But some of her servants seem to have been most faithfully attached to her and to her husband, even after the war.

The mother of six children naturally gives a great part of her life to them. Mrs. Davis was faithful and devoted. "I feel the responsibilities of a parent so intensely," she says, "that I thank God that there is a time when the power, and consequently the onus of failure ceases." [10] She enjoyed her children, and admired and praised them, as a loyal parent should. I appreciate also the somewhat franker expression of actuality which comes out in a letter to the father: "Billy is well but bad. Jeff is unremunerative, but behaves well in the main." [11] Few mothers could have been put to a severer test than that hurried, horrible flight from Richmond, with four helpless children, the youngest a baby of only a year. Mrs. Davis stood it admirably, and in later illnesses and suffering her devotion was beautifully constant. Few mothers, also, have to go through the tragedy of five deaths. Mrs. Davis endured it and lived, but with what agony may be imagined. Like Mrs. Lincoln in Washington, she lost a son while she was in the White House at Richmond. Little Joe fell from the second story upon a brick pavement and was killed. First we have the earlier picture of the child trotting into

169

the parlor among visitors in his nightgown to say his prayers at his father's knee. Then close upon this comes Mrs. Chesnut's dramatic account of the funeral: "Here I see that funeral procession as it wound among those tall white monuments, up the hillside, the James River tumbling about below over rocks and around islands; the dominant figure that poor, old, gray-haired man, standing, bareheaded, straight as an arrow, clear against the sky, by the open grave of his son. She, the bereft mother, stood back, in her heavy black wrappings, and her tall figure drooped. The flowers, the children, the procession as it moved, comes and goes, but those two dark, sorrow-stricken figures stand: they are before me now." [12]

It is clear that Mrs. Davis must have had a superb physique to go through all she did. There were brief moments when she gave out. After pulling Billy from the very grip of death, she lay for three weeks "on the sofa helpless and with my pulse so low that I felt an almost utter unability to be either glad or sorry." [13] But in the main she was vigorous and energetic, equal to all efforts and to all emergencies.

Also, she had God with her always. The comfort of religion was an immense support to her and to her husband, both. In early years Davis himself seems to have had some intellectual difficulties. But after a long period of quiet plantation life, with much thinking and reading, he came out with a sharp and literal orthodoxy, the limits of which are perhaps best revealed to modern Northern readers in his passionate defense of the great Southern institution: "When the low and vulgar son of Noah, who laughed at his father's exposure, sunk by debasing himself and his lineage by a connection with an inferior race of men, he doomed his descendants to perpetual slavery." [14] General Schaff justly and ingeniously connects this narrow, dogmatic theological standpoint of the Confederate President with the solitude and remoteness of his youthful surroundings. It is curious to reflect that Professor Stephenson, with equal justice, has found in the same background, working on a different temperament, much of the origin of Lincoln's dreamy and poetical mysticism.

Davis's religious attitude and preoccupation were not wholly acceptable to some of his critics. Their feeling about it appears in the bitter comment of the *Richmond Examiner*: "We find the President standing in a corner telling his beads and relying on a miracle to save the country." [15] Even more significant is the pointed comment of Davis's own little boy, when his mother invited him at a critical

171

moment to come and pray, "You had better have my pony saddled, and let me go out to help father; we can pray afterward." [16] Nevertheless, there is something genuinely impressive and winning about the intense sincerity and earnestness of Davis's religion, as shown in his long conversations with Doctor Craven, and Mrs. Davis turned as constantly as he did to the comfort which is most unfailing for those who can find it. When the clouds hung darkest about her, she wrote: "However, we hope all things and trust in God as the only one able to resolve the opposite state of feeling into a triumphant, happy whole." [17]

II

For a woman who plays such a great part in the world as Mrs. Davis did, the social life is necessarily the most conspicuous, if not the most important. Mrs. Davis had some eminent social qualities. She liked to meet people, she liked to watch them and analyze them. She could talk brilliantly and attractively with almost anyone. She could make her house run easily and could furnish an excellent table, even when the resources for such a purpose were somewhat scanty. She dressed with taste and elegance. She was dignified and imposing, and affected all sorts of people by her personality, sometimes favorably, sometimes not quite so much so. Pollard, who detested her, gives a description which is savage, not to say brutal: "Mrs. Davis was a brawny, able-bodied woman, who had much more of masculine mettle than of feminine grace. Her complexion was tawny, even to the point of mulattoism; a woman loud and coarse in her manners; full of self-assertion." [18] The gentle General Schaff suggests something bewilderingly different: She "had soft, liquid, dark eyes, a voice of Southern charm, and was a ready, pleasing talker." [19] Perhaps Mr. Eckenrode's medium view is the most just: "She was rather handsome, though her features were slightly marred by a thick upper lip which gave her, unjustly, a slight suggestion of cruelty. It was a smooth, proud, comely face." [20]

As to Mrs. Davis's ease and vivacity in conversation there is little dispute. She held her own with the best talkers in Washington and drew out the best they had. She is said to have been sarcastic. Such a quick tongue cannot always escape that charge. She sometimes allowed her sense of the comic to get the better of her amiability. One day a lady who was supervising the cutting out of undergarments for the soldiers, complained almost with tears that by an unfortunate mistake all the

drawers had been cut out for one leg. The other
ladies present listened with considerate sympathy;
but Mrs. Davis laughed loud and long.[21] Yet her
sketches of the great characters about her, as they
appear in her book, are remarkably free from harshness or satire, though the temptation to it must
often have been great. What the quick quality of
her wit was I find nicely suggested in the brief
exchange which she reports between herself and
Secretary Benjamin, though her object was rather
to bring out his quickness than hers. She had dis-
agreed with him on some trivial point and declined
to argue about it. "I playfully said, 'If I let you
set one stone, you will build a cathedral.' He
laughed and answered, 'If it should prove to be the
shrine of truth, you will worship there with me, I
am sure.' " [22]

With these social gifts and limitations, Mrs.
Davis obtained a considerable success during the
Washington years. No one speaks of her exactly
with enthusiasm; but her cleverness drew all sorts
of people about her, and her intelligence held them.
Her intimate discussion of men of all parties and
pursuits proves how wide was her acquaintance with
them, and her husband's popularity insured her ac-
cess to any circle that she cared to enter. Mrs.
Pryor says: "Nor must we fail to acknowledge the

social influence of Mrs. Jefferson Davis, one of the most brilliant women of her time—greatly sought by cultivated men and women." [23]

But when it came to the social leadership of the Confederacy during those critical days in Richmond, it was a different matter. Mrs. Davis had to encounter precisely the same difficulties that Mrs. Lincoln met in Washington. If she lived simply and unpretentiously, as her husband was anxious to do and himself persistently did, the critics complained that she was not keeping up the social dignity of her position, was narrow, exclusive, and regardless of popular interest. If she tried to entertain, there was an immediate outcry that the White House was callous to the sufferings and disasters of the country. The trouble was aggravated by Davis's limitations of strength. He declared that he could not be a social and an administrative officer at the same time, and the latter function seemed more important. Mrs. Davis met the situation as best she could. She gave some public receptions, which were well attended and successful, in spite of unkind comments. She received more informally in the evening and gathered around her the most brilliant and interesting people to be found in the Confederate capital. But there was always plenty of fault-finding. The *Examiner* shrieked over the White House display and luxury. The President had costly horses and carriages and entertained expensively, while the poor people of the South were suffering.[24] Mrs. Davis was extravagant, loved ostentation, and cared little for the misery that was so evident everywhere about her.

These charges were no doubt exaggerated and unjust. At the same time, it is clear that neither Davis nor his wife had the gift of being democratically popular. They both had a strong sense of the dignity of their position and were apt to emphasize it in tactless ways. One little story is told, not directly affecting Mrs. Davis, but vividly illustrating the atmosphere she developed about her. "It was usual for the Howell girls of President Davis's family to come into church after the service had begun, and, beautifully gowned, to walk down the aisle to the President's pew in front of the chancel. On this Sunday Mrs. General Lee, who was in town, came to church before the service began. She was very plainly dressed, and, being recognized by the sexton, was taken at once by the usher to the President's pew. When, later, the Howell girls marched down the aisle to the pew, they observed this plain old woman . . . and stood at the door of the pew for her to vacate. Instantly there was a hiss all over the church. Every near-by pew door was thrown open to Mrs. Lee." [25] The narrative continues, perhaps not very plausibly, to state that the next week Davis called on General Lee to apologize, and Lee's somewhat dry remark was: "I assure you it makes no difference as it is. If, however, it had been some poor, obscure woman of the neighborhood, it would have been a serious mistake." Such incidents were not very helpful to Mrs. Davis's public career.

Moreover, even for a more adaptable temperament, the conditions in Richmond would have been somewhat trying. The old Virginia aristocracy was never particularly lenient towards outsiders.[26] Mrs. Chesnut, who was a most charming person and came from South Carolina, where good society had some opinion of itself, complains rather bitterly of the tone at the capital: "Until we came here we had never heard of our social position. We do not know how to be rude to people who call. To talk of social position seems vulgar. Down our way that sort of thing was settled one way or another beyond a peradventure, like the earth and the sky. We never gave it a thought. We talked to whom we pleased, and if they were not *comme il faut,* we were ever so much more polite to the poor things. No reflections on Virginia: everybody comes to Richmond." [27] Now the President and his wife came from a much more doubtful region than South Carolina. At first Richmond society was inclined to be tolerant and good-natured, and a thoroughly tactful and conciliatory disposition might have overcome all prejudice. Mrs. Davis had not such a disposition. The feeling which grew up about her is well indicated in a letter written me by a Southern lady of to-day: "I wonder if your pen can invest that I almost said hybrid opportunist with the glamour of interest and romance. I never cared for her and I believe the older Southern people who were in a position to know did not care for her, either. She wasn't a Southern woman, and while we may admire her loyalty to her husband and her adopted cause and country, we realize it was self-interest rather than simon-pure patriotism that actuated her." Yet even Nero had flowers placed upon his grave by an unknown hand. And when the exigencies of the time forced Mrs. Davis to sell her horses, an anonymous purchaser returned them to her stables the next morning.[28] So I fancy some people loved her, after all.

She had evidently the impulsive generosity and sympathy which belong to a quick, ill-regulated, impetuous nature. She did not do much visiting in the hospitals, which were naturally such a prominent element in Richmond life, giving the rather

178

singular reason that "Mr. Davis felt it was best for me not to expose the men to the restraint my presence might have imposed." [29] I doubt whether sustained self-sacrifice would have come easy to her or have often been accepted. Yet there are many little touches of kindness, unobtrusive but obviously sincere, which show that there was a human heart in her somewhere. Above all, she was capable of warm and tender affection where she had once attached herself. No study of her would be complete that did not take into account the really lovely letters written to Mrs. Howell Cobb in the disastrous years after the war. There is far more than a merely perfunctory regard conveyed in passages like the following: "I so often think of you surrounded by children and grandchildren, a home and a future, and bless God that all I love are not like me, floating uprooted. Do, dear old friend, write to me and tell me *every little* thing about yourself and your family. I am so much afraid of your feeling yourself a stranger to me, and of each cord becoming loosened by disuse, until we drop off altogether into that mechanical intercourse, valueless because labored. . . . Maggie and Mr. Davis send love to you and your dear children, and dear, reliable, old, tender friend, I

am, as ever—." [30]   Surely the woman who wrote
that was lovable as well as loving.

III

But the warmth of Mrs. Davis's affection was in
the main bestowed upon her husband, and the depth
and constancy of their mutual love are quite beyond
dispute. Davis had naturally a tender and devoted
temperament and the kind of temperament that
concentrates its tenderness upon one object. His
first marriage, to the daughter of Zachary Taylor,
was romantic in its persistence against the opposition of the bride's father and in the tragic circumstances of her early death by the infectious fever
which almost killed her husband. Mrs. Varina
Davis's account of her predecessor is worth quoting
as an instance of tact in the handling of a rather
difficult matter: "Though a woman of great decision of character, she was devoid of the least
trace of stubbornness; her judgment was mature,
her nature open and faithful, and her temper affectionate and responsive." [31] You could hardly praise
with more discriminating sincerity and less pre-
tentiousness.

When Davis made his second choice, he did it
with loyal and abundant affection, and his attach-

ment to Varina showed in all the crises of his life
as well as in the ordinary current of it. Here again
Pollard is worth quoting for the extreme hostile
view: "Mr. Davis was the most uxorious of men;
and it was surprising that a man of his fine nervous
organism . . . should have fallen so much under
the dominion of a woman, who was excessively
coarse and physical in her person, and in whom
the defects of nature had been repaired neither by
the grace of manners nor the charms of conversation." [32] Extravagant and absurd as this is, it well
indicates the devotion which Davis himself repeatedly expressed. In the height of triumph and success he turned to the one person with whom he
wished to share them. In failure and despair he
poured out his soul to her, and her tenderness
and sympathy were his greatest consolation. Speaking to Doctor Craven, during the long days of captivity, he made clear this attitude under the form
of general appraisal of woman's helpfulness:
"Beautiful as woman's character always was, in its
purity, grace, delicacy, and sympathetic action, it
was rarely, save in man's hours of deepest affliction,
that he realized how much he stood in need of the
support of his gentle counterpart." [33] In the long
and elaborate letter, written in April, 1865, just
after the great downfall, he expresses his marital

181

affection with touching directness and intensity.
He has made and will make every sacrifice but one,
which is beyond him: "I have sacrificed so much
for the cause of the Confederacy that I can measure
my ability to make any further sacrifice required,
and am assured there is but one to which I am not
equal—my wife and my children." [34] He recognizes
that, instead of the great hopes that had been held
out to her, he has little left to offer; but he knows
that she loves him for himself and not what he can
bring: "Dear wife, this is not the fate to which I
invited you when the future was rose colored to
us both; but I know you will bear it even better
than myself, and that, of us two, I alone will ever
look back reproachfully on my past career." [35] And
he assures her at least of his undying devotion, such
as it is: "Farewell, my dear, there may be better
things in store for us than are now in view, but my
love is all I have to offer, and that has the value
of a thing long possessed, and sure not to be lost." [36]

Mrs. Davis's response to this affection was
equally devoted and self-forgetful. Strong, self-
reliant, and dominating she may have been. But
she was a woman and a lover, and I like especially
her confession of longing and dependence when she
at last receives permission to correspond with her
imprisoned and tormented husband: "The permis-

sion has relieved me of the dreadful sense of loneliness and agonizing doubt and weight of responsibility. I may ask his advice instead of acting upon my own suggestions, and above all I may know from him how he is." [37] The same warm note of passionate tenderness sounds through all her letters and her book.

And that book is the heart of the matter in dealing with Mrs. Davis. Among these various studies of wives this is the only case in which a wife has written formally and elaborately about her husband. It seems almost cruel to take advantage when the game is played so directly into your hand. Yet if we are trying to study the husband and the wife, both, we cannot overlook such significant aid when it is offered us. Evidently there are few tasks more difficult for a woman to undertake than to write about her husband, though many women plunge into it with entire serenity. In one sense it may be said that a woman who knows a man in his daily home life—a mother, a wife, a sister, a daughter—knows him better than anyone else can. When he goes out into the world and deals with other men—and women, it may be urged that he puts on a mask which he drops completely by the domestic hearth. But, after all, that mask is part of the man. The outside counts as well as the inside. And that outside the wife rarely sees as the outer world sees it. She knows much that the world knows not; but some things the world sees that she is ignorant of, and of which no one gives her an inkling.

Further, a wife usually knows many of her husband's defects; no one better. She has the keenest insight into them, and is often ready enough to point them out—to him. But when it comes to telling outsiders, it is another matter. Not only loyalty to him, but her own pride and self-respect impel, oblige her to cover up, to defend, to deal in the cunning alchemy of love which transforms defects into curious excellences. She may be aware of this process or she may not; it is hard to say which state of mind more impairs the validity of her testimony.

But, try as she will, she cannot tell the life-story without making the defects stand out. The more she conceals, extenuates, excuses, the weaker her case is apt to become. The more passionately she idolizes and defends her hero, the greater is the danger that the indifferent reader will find her gently ridiculous and the kindly reader pathetic, while the very efforts she makes to exalt the idol are apt to result in damaging him in a manner far, far different from what she anticipated. Perhaps I may again quote in connection with Mrs. Davis the beautiful

184

lines of Beaumont which I applied long ago to Mrs. Longstreet's *Life* of her distinguished husband:

> "Those have most power to hurt us that we love:
> We lay our sleeping lives within their arms." [38]

It cannot be denied that, granting the difficulty of the undertaking, Mrs. Davis has done her work with great skill. She herself sets a very high standard and one that few can expect to attain: "Detraction is the easiest form of criticism or eloquence, but just, discriminating praise requires the presence in the commentators of many of those qualities which are commended in the subject." [39] In general she avoids foolish and unfounded eulogy and she endeavors at least to meet and dispose of intelligent criticism. In any case she tells us much of value about her husband and about herself. Only the discerning reader gathers a great deal of this without any intention on the writer's part.

One is struck first with Mrs. Davis's insistence upon her husband's health. For all his activity, for all his exposure to hardship and endurance of it in his military life, he seems always to have been sensitive, to have been liable to illness; and in later years, that is during his Senatorship and Presidency, he suffered intensely and frequently. His nervous susceptibility to pain and distress in others was so extreme that he could not even endure to have the story of the Babes in the Wood read to him when he was ill. Through all his physical trials Mrs. Davis tended him with devoted care. At least it appears so from her narrative, and no one disputes it. In one illness, when he was threatened with the loss of an eye and the doctors wondered how it could possibly have escaped, he said, "My wife saved it." And the wife's comment is, "All the triumphs of my life were and are concentrated in and excelled by this blessed memory." [40] Mrs. Davis insists upon the patience, the fortitude, the cheerfulness with which her husband endured all these afflictions. He did not allow them to affect his temper, she says. Yet one finds it hard to believe that a great ruler of men could be made out of such material.

Take another aspect of Davis's character, his intelligence. His wife emphasizes with perfect justice the clear and high and broad quality of this. He thought widely and deeply about many things, especially things political, reasoned forcibly, and put the process of his reasoning in vivid and effective form. But when he had once arrived at conclusions, he would not readily change them; when he had definitely established his own standpoint, it was extremely difficult for him to recognize that

there could be any other. This defect seriously
hampered his whole career. And his wife has
brought it out with entire clearness. When she
first meets him, long before there was any thought
of marriage, her shrewd insight discerns the flaw.
"He impresses me as a remarkable kind of man,
but of uncertain temper, and has a way of taking
for granted that everybody agrees with him when
he expresses an opinion, which offends me." [41]
Later, after better knowledge, she reiterates her
feeling of the limitation, even in passionate defense:
"He sincerely thought all he said, and, moreover,
could not understand any other man coming to a
different conclusion after his premises were stated.
It was this sincerity of opinion which sometimes
gave him the manner to which his opponents objected as domineering." [42] And friends objected
to it as well as opponents.

The dogmatic, positive, fixed attitude which
showed itself in abstract intellectual matters was
still more obtrusive and damaging in the management of men. Mrs. Davis insists, again with entire
justice, upon Davis's tenderness and kindness. He
wished no one to suffer. Suffering irritated him,
and he endeavored to relieve it wherever he could.
Moreover, he was very sensitive to the opinions of
others: "Every shade of feeling that crossed the

minds of those about him was noticed, and he could not bear anyone to be inimical to him." [43] But he moved in an atmosphere of high thought and settled conviction, where there was little room for the wishes and plans and convictions of others. There is one striking phrase of Mrs. Davis's, not written in connection with her husband, but having a certain bearing upon him, all the same: "Perhaps I attach too much importance to the humanism of great men, but I have observed that this quality is oftenest found wanting in men of great intellect." [44] It was humanism that was wanting in Davis, for all his sensibility. He was not adaptable, not pliable. He wanted no one about him but those who shared his views or at least submitted to them. It was difficult for him to use great instruments according to their own quality for great purposes. In this, as in many other points, he has a notable resemblance to Woodrow Wilson. It was this spiritual rigidity which involved Davis in his tragic and fatal quarrels with Joseph E. Johnston, with Beauregard, with Toombs, and with many others. And then we have Mrs. Davis's pitifully characteristic remark in regard to one minor incident: "The talent for governing men without humiliating them, which Mr. Davis had in an eminent degree, cannot be acquired, it is inborn." [45] These are the methods of defense which drive one's perversity almost to the assertion of the opposite: he had the talent for humiliating men without governing them. Truly, those have most power to hurt us that we love.

So everywhere the worshiping wife urges good qualities that are undeniable in themselves; but she does not see that often the excess of these qualities becomes defect. She praises her husband's sincerity. He was admirably sincere; but an outspoken frankness may bruise and wound. And she proclaims him loyal. So he was, always. But the loyalty too often meant a mistaken and perverse clinging to servants and supporters who were unworthy. And no doubt there are other qualities less ambiguous and disputable, and in enlarging upon these Mrs. Davis has the agreement and sympathy of everyone. Her husband's courage was fine and undisputed. No one can question his readiness for sacrifice. No one can question his instinct of patriotism, his persistent devotion to the cause he had undertaken to serve. The devotion may have been misdirected; it was absolutely and constantly sincere. Yet it is curious that at the very end of her long narrative Mrs. Davis, without in the least meaning to do so, makes perhaps the severest criticism that can be made by anyone. Many historical students to-day are inclined to hold that from the beginning the Confederate cause was hopeless, that no man, however gifted, occupying the place of Jefferson Davis, could have brought about a different result, though the various aspects of the struggle might have been altered. Yet Mrs. Davis, quite unconsciously, places the burden of failure not upon the inherent impossibility of success, but upon causes in the nature of the man himself: "In the greatest effort of his life, Mr. Davis failed from the predominance of some of these noble qualities." [46] Again I say, those have most power to hurt us that we love.

Yet, whatever the hurt or the help of her defense and criticism, no one can dispute the wife's absorbing, enduring affection. Her husband was all in all to her, and she had little hope, little interest, little thought for anything else. She shared his triumphs, she comforted his weakness, she cheered his captivity so far as she could, and when she could not she made every possible effort, even to the point of humiliation, for his release. Whatever her defects, and they were many and obvious, she was a devoted wife, and the last words of a passionate letter, written in the moment of greatest peril, sum up all that is finest and most winning about her: "Oh, my dearest, precious husband, the one absorbing love of my whole life, may God keep you from harm." [47]

IV

Mrs. Davis's communion with her husband was not only a personal and domestic matter. There was no aspect of his career, no phase of his activity, in which she was not interested. She was always a considerable reader, and it is evident that she had read and thought and talked on political affairs, abstractly as well as in detail, in a way to make her a suggestive and interesting companion. The knowledge of all the elements of the great struggle displayed in her book is really astonishing. She constantly helped her husband, acting as his secretary, and writing both for him and with him. Her Northern antecedents and connections rendered her somewhat suspicious to critical Southerners, as Mrs. Lincoln was in Washington. But there cannot be a moment's doubt of her passionate sympathy with the Confederate cause. Only she was shrewd enough to see, especially toward the end, what her husband's rigorous logic was so reluctant to admit, the hopeless contradiction between the theory of State Rights, on which the Confederacy was founded, and the stern exigencies of military control. Writing to a friend just when the catastrophe was near, she frankly expresses her heresy in this regard: "The cohesive power of a strong government is needed when the disintegrating tendency of misery is at work. The consent of the masses governed is only accorded to government which confers at that time large blessings—faith is never displayed by the masses in things hoped for if they chance to be those every-day blessings which we call necessaries—I am disheartened with popular sovereignty, still more with State sovereignty, and fear both are fallacies." [48] Which at least suffices to show that she was a woman who thought, and thought keenly.

With such political thinking and with her temperament, it would be natural to assume that she had a great influence over her husband. Unquestionably she had. To be sure, Davis disliked political women. He told Doctor Craven that woman's "true altar is the happy fireside, not the forum with its foul breath and distracting clamors." [49] Nevertheless, his intimate letters show how freely he talked everything over with his wife, and his enemies believed that her influence was constant and far from beneficial. Mr. Eckenrode probably puts the matter in the fairest light: "There can be no doubt that Varina Davis was a congenial companion for an intellectual man, and that she secured a considerable influence over her husband, even possibly in political matters. Her abounding vitality would have made her predominant over the semi-invalid Davis but for a will which always kept him master of himself." [50]

In technical military affairs the influence would of course be less felt. Yet the ample discussion of these in the *Life* shows how fully Mrs. Davis was conversant with them, and during his occasional absences Davis writes to her with abundant detail of military events and extended comment upon them, proving at least that she understood all that was going on. In the long and most curious letter, written April 7, 1865, Mrs. Davis strikingly reveals her attitude as to the incidents of the war and the men concerned in it. Here you trace with the greatest nicety the character of her influence and just the form in which it was exerted: "Though I know you do not like my interference, let me entreat you not to send B. B. [Braxton Bragg] to command there, I am satisfied that the country will be ruined by its intestine feuds if you do so. . . . If I am intrusive, forgive me for the sake of the love which impels me, but pray long and fervently before you decide to do it." [51] No one will deny that this is tactfully expressed.

As regards more general public policy it might be expected that Mrs. Davis's opinion would be even more decided and her advice more urgent. How close, how intimate, how constant was her watchfulness as to what went on appears admirably in her own rather remarkable admission that "she was an auditor in an adjoining room when the Cabinet met to hear the report of the Commissioners" who brought back word from the vital conference in Hampton Roads.[52] The sentence which Pollard quotes as to the project to make Lee commander-in-chief may not be literal, but its vehemence is by no means uncharacteristic: "I think I am the person to advise Mr. Davis; and if I were he, I would die or be hung before I would submit to the humiliation that Congress intended him."[53] Much more impressive, however, because more in the spirit of the military passage above cited, is the bit from the letter of April 28, 1865, referring to the last despairing hope of transferring the Confederate government beyond the Mississippi: "As to the trans-Mississippi, I doubt if at first things will be straight, but the spirit is there, and the daily accretions will be great when the deluded of this side are crushed out between the upper and nether millstone. But you have now tried the 'strict construction' fallacy. If we are to require a Constitution, it must be much stretched during our hours of outside pressure if it covers us at all." [54] Surely this was a masterful woman, and one who might herself have dreamed of building empires.

There were also unpleasant stories of much more personal interference with the progress of national affairs. Mrs. Davis had violent prejudices, as, for that matter, had her husband. It was rumored that these prejudices had more to do with the making and marring of military officials, great and little, than actual merit. Such stories are apt to arise without much foundation, but it will hardly be denied that something in Mrs. Davis's character and bearing gave them color. It was currently believed that to be connected with the presidential household meant sure promotion and support. And again this is a usual form of slander; but the bitter sentence of the *Richmond Examiner* no doubt expresses a widespread popular indignation: If the President's secretary "will only take the trouble to inform us what one of the President's family and of the late General Taylor's is not holding office anywhere, we shall not only print it with pleasure, but the public will receive this information with a gratification heightened by surprise." [55]

Yet in spite of all these activities and interests and efforts, I am inclined to think that Mrs. Davis had less personal ambition than might be imagined. She would have been active and assertive in any sphere of life; but she would have been equally contented, perhaps more so, in a humbler domestic career. She herself sums up the drawbacks, with her usual keenness: "Then I began to know the bitterness of being a politician's wife, and that it meant long absences, pecuniary depletion from ruinous absenteeism, illness from exposure, misconceptions, defamation of character — everything which darkens the sunlight and contracts the happy sphere of home." [56] And if it be said that this was written in age and to a certain extent for public effect, we may turn to the charming passage, responding to a remark of her husband's which I have quoted above: "It is surely not the fate to which you invited me in brighter days, but you must remember that you did not invite me to a great hero's home, but to that of a plain farmer. I have shared all your triumphs, been the *only* beneficiary of them; now I am but claiming the privilege for the first time of being all to you." [57]

At any rate, what ambition she had was altogether merged in her husband's, and she herself insists, and with apparent justice, that his ambition was less than some people suppose. He did not want the Presidency, she says, would have preferred a military command, and this is commonly believed, though Mrs. Davis's talk with Mrs. Keckley before the war would seem to indicate that even then the headship of the Confederacy was looked upon as almost certain.[58] In Davis's case it is a little difficult to separate personal ambition from the tremendous, dogged, driving determination to make his cause and his policy and his splendid, insistent will triumph over all the obstacles of a perverse and wicked world. He had God with him, he must triumph, he would triumph, and she would help him triumph. Then he failed, disastrously, ruinously, and the world tumbled to pieces about him and her. The hopes, the desires, the efforts, the maddening sacrifices of four bitter years culminated in a calamity which in the beginning had seemed to her absolutely unthinkable. There was the hurried flight South, the nightmare capture in the gray dawn, the agonized uncertainty of imprisonment and trial, the Odyssey of exile and privation, the loss of the idol who had meant the whole of life to her, and the long later years filled with the immense brooding shadow of a great memory. Mrs. Davis's life ends for us with the death of her husband. In spite of later activities and experiences, no doubt she would have wished it to end actually, in the spirit of the beautiful passage in one of her letters to Mrs. Cobb: "I watch over him unceasingly and pray to go first if it must be that we are to be parted. Twenty years' difference asserts itself, when the younger of the two is middle-aged, and I am in terror whenever he leaves me." [59] But if she had expressed such a wish to him, he might have answered with the words of Hamlet to Horatio:

> "Absent thee from felicity a while,
> And in this harsh world draw thy breath in pain,
> To tell my story."

And she did tell it, with all the life she had and all she had had, with all her loves and all her hates and all her hopes and all her dreams.

VII

MRS. BENJAMIN F. BUTLER

CHRONOLOGY

Sarah Hildreth Butler.
Born, Dracut, Massachusetts, August 17, 1816.
Married Benjamin F. Butler, May 16, 1844.
Died, April 8, 1876.

MRS. BENJAMIN F. BUTLER

I

MRS. BUTLER is known through printed material during only a few years of her life with her husband and in the most intimate connection with him. She was born in 1816, in the small town of Dracut, Massachusetts, the daughter of a physician named Hildreth. She had a passion for the drama and Shakespeare, studied for the stage and acted for a short time, then left it to marry the young lawyer of Lowell. She had a numerous family, led a busy, useful life, and died in 1876. There is no biography of her, no elaborate record coming from herself or others. But a large number of her letters from 1860 to 1865 are printed in connection with her husband's. They are letters of extraordinary brilliancy and force of self-revelation, and they give a startling, varied, and veracious likeness of a most original and interesting spirit.

It is best first to establish this striking couple in the normal current of happy and fortunate mar-

ried life, the substantial and sympathetic sharing
of common suffering and common joy. It is evident that, at any rate during the years when we
know them, they were well off. There were ample
means for comfortable and even luxurious living.
Money was always abundant and there is no sign
of the wear and tear so sure to accompany financial
stringency. There was a large and beautiful house
in Lowell, plenty of servants, horses and carriages,
and all the equipment of a man and woman prominent in the community and able to appear so.
Everywhere there is the sense of ease, of the ability and the disposition to have the external bene-
fits which do not make happiness, but go far to
sustain it. "Do not neglect your dinners," writes
Mrs. Butler to her sister at home; "go down with
the children and get nice sweetbreads or some
agreeable tit-bits such as you and the children like,
and take some little pains about it, for after all
the daily comforts of life should not be overlooked." [1] They were not, and in consequence
home was a pleasant place, and the wife could
write securely to her husband of her desire to have
him return to it: "What happiness it would be
to see you coming up the avenue, even *greater*
that there would be none to greet you but me.
We should not say much, happy enough to sit

down together and look on one of the loveliest views in nature, satisfied that this is home." [2]

And if home was happy and comfortable, it was not only money, but still more her thought and gift, that made it so. It is clear that she was an admirable domestic manager, understood the elaborate art of household economy in all its developments, and knew how to make the machinery run smoothly, with no evidence of machinery at all. That this could not be accomplished without effort she understood well enough, if others did not: "You would be amazed to know how closely my time is occupied, and yet I do nothing. Other people with their calls, wants, and troubles take up my time." [3] But she accomplished it. It is delightful, when she is absent, to see the care and forethought with which she plans what is to be done at home, what is to be cared for, what may not be neglected. With servants it is manifest that she has kindness and sympathy. Her attitude is human always: "With a mixture of firmness and kindliness you may be able to get along with him comfortably." [4] But she proposes to have the work done and done well. "Now I think of it," she writes to her husband, "tell Stephen to clean your tents more thoroughly. . . . He needs scolding." [5] With the intense domestic energy of the true New England housewife, she no sooner gets into even a temporary dwelling, but she takes steps to put it in order: "I could not help putting this house in order, new carpeting the entry and stairs, and taking up the others to have them cleaned." [6]

In all these things Mrs. Butler is perfectly and charmingly a woman. She is so likewise in her social instinct and the elements that go with it. Without the least trace of vanity or coquetry, she knew that she had beauty, made suitable efforts to preserve it, and sighed for the possible loss of it. She quotes a friend's ecstasy over charms that have vanished with youth and regrets them—because her husband may: "I lie here so pale and wearied, so unattractive, that I would fain present some bright season of life when I was looked at with pleasure, and *loved,* by those who felt the inspiration of my nature." [7] She liked dress, too, enjoyed pretty things, and her letters have just such references to them as is normal and proper: "What became of the pearls, . . . ? I think ladies can never hear of such pretty baubles without a desire to behold them, and it is apt to increase with indulgence." [8]

She employed all these minor agencies, in combination with greater ones, to achieve social success, and it is clear that she did achieve it. Men and

MRS. BENJAMIN F. BUTLER

women liked her because she understood them, sympathized with them, and went out of her way to do those little kindnesses that seem insignificant and yet go so far. It is said that both she and her daughter were immensely popular with the common soldiers, and I can well believe it, and this went a good way towards solidifying the popularity of her husband. She was quite aware of her gifts in this direction, and meant to use them, every one. When important personages come to headquarters, she entertains them luxuriously and flatters herself that she "did it for once with a good deal of skill." [9] At any rate, her husband believed in her social powers. He begs her to conciliate and charm Mrs. Grant: "If you do all that your knowledge of the world, tact, and genius will enable you to do, then you will do a thousand times more in captivating the woman than I could possibly do with the husband." [10]

Of intimate friends outside her own family there is not much suggestion in these letters. Mrs. Butler may have had them; during the war period she was too busy to give them much of her life. But those who were closely connected with her had claims that were never disregarded. She was deeply attached to her brother and sisters, and her devotion to her dying sister is eminently pathetic. She was sensitive to all suffering and misery, and grief over the wounded in the hospitals depresses and unnerves her: "I called for Mrs. Usher and went over to the hospital. I am afraid to go alone, and when I get there I shrink from going in, for fear they will think I go only from curiosity. Oh, they are a sad sight—crippled, maimed for life, and many with death standing beside them." [11] Energetic, self-sustained, well-balanced as she was, all this crowding burden of the varied world sometimes overcomes her, and she cries out for peace—and love: "I get so wearied and nervous with the varying cares that if there is not absolute peace between you and me, *somewhere, to rest*—I falter at once and sink down presently, bruised and helpless—till the daily routine hurries me on again, to care for the many that come." [12]

Yes, for all the happy background, in that tremendous crisis of national and personal struggle, there could not but be many weary and discouraged hours, hours when it seemed as if the nerves and muscles would positively and finally refuse to do their duty. "I am in that state of nervous irritation that I cannot endure to think on one thing for five minutes." [13] And so fatigue and ill-health have their normal place in the letters, as they have in life. He has his times of illness, and she is anxious about

206

him, anxious to take care of him, anxious as to how he will be taken care of. She has her own times of illness, when for the moment even she has to give up. But she is at it again quickly, for there is not a trace of the shirk about her; on the contrary, she is bound to die fighting, if die she must: "In truth, I could sink down, wearied, only that that is a poor resource, not fit for a thinking, earnest man or woman." [14]

She had her higher forms of refuge also, to which she could escape when the daily strain and turmoil got too much for her. She had a broad, lucid intelligence, and liked to use it at all times. Beauty appealed to her and consoled her, not so much, perhaps, beauty of painting or music—at least she makes little reference to these—but beauty of literature and the splendor of the great poets. Also, she is exquisitely alive to the charm of nature and has really magical words for rendering it. Storms thrill her and enchant her, and she watches the movement of the swallows or the martins through them and before them, delightedly.[15] Then a calm night sets her dreaming, and all she asks is love to share it: "Such a flood of light and beauty you never gazed on. The moon is full—the wind cool and fragrant, waving the long, pendent willows that float like a woman's hair on the sighing breeze. The long dark shadows sweep over the lawn and roads. It is not calm and still. The deep sighs and whispering among the trees make it a night of strange, mysterious beauty. The air is alive with spirits, agitated with sudden news; they float tremulously in and out among the trees like phantoms as they are. I feel, in gazing, as though I belonged to them, and could easily pass the space and put my hands upon your shoulders and look you in the face. I wonder if you would start back from me, or naturally fold me in your arms. I shall find out by my dreams to-night." [16]

Then there was God, an even surer refuge for spent nerves and weary spirits. But God is not especially prominent in these letters of Mrs. Butler. She may have been settled on the fundamentals, but she hardly retained the childish simplicity of faith, much more than her husband retained it. With his glib tongue and facile memory, he was always citing Scripture for his purposes, too often with the unfortunate lack of taste which so fatally characterized him. But it is doubtful if the impressions went very deep. His wife feels his skepticism and tries to stir him out of it: "For you will yet believe, time will bring faith, that the love that has absorbed the highest and noblest emotions of our nature is yet a spark from heaven that will glow with finer glory when it has passed the ordeal of earth." [17] When she is considering joining the church, he puts no difficulties in her way, but frankly confesses that he cannot share her faith: "If I *could* believe, I would become a member of the church, but, alas! I haven't faith. You may have." [18] But when it comes to the point of decision, she doubts and hesitates. In an admirable passage of thoughtful debate, she examines her attitude. "I have always been more a believer than a skeptic. Christ is the only perfect model I have ever read of. . . . Man as we find him now is no such being. . . . No one can live a day without some unworthy thought, some act or speech that they would be unwilling to trace, or have traced to its true cause. So that if the conscience is ever honest with itself, repentance must follow, and remission of sins can be given only by some being possessing those attributes that we ascribe to Christ." [19] Yet still, still she is not ready for the complete surrender: "I have a great dread of doing anything hypocritical, and many things that I am not now aware of might come up to make me feel that I was out of place." [20]

The harmony between husband and wife was even less disturbed in earthly relations than in heavenly. They both were devoted to their children and took great comfort and satisfaction in them, and the children did them credit. The daughter, Blanche, inherited her mother's beauty and much of her mother's varied attraction and charm. Mrs. Butler's letters are full of references to the children's welfare. She is solicitous about their health, their education, their clothing, and their future. As she reads that of her daughter from her own, she feels a mixture of foreboding and hope: "She will see things more charming, rich, and clothed with a dreamy beauty, sometimes in her life, and she will be more worried, troubled, and shaken with grief at others. So the balance will be about even. But if I were to choose for her, I would have her jolly and selfish." [21] At all times she feels a deep sympathy with them, interprets their joys and sorrows from her own memories: "Children cannot express, but they feel as keenly as grown people." [22] Yet dear and close to her as the children are, they are forgotten in a profounder, tenderer attachment, and when she is parting from her husband even the thought of home cannot console her: "You will not be surprised at this deep sadness which held me even up to our own gate, without one throb of pleasant expectation at sight of home and all it contains until I heard the sound of the children's voices playing in the evergreens." [23]

II

For under the varied current of normal, daily life, the one thing that counts in her existence is the love for Benjamin F. Butler, and the longing to have him love her in return. This love, and the singular gift of subtle self-analysis with which she depicts it, make her correspondence a high-wrought romance, tortured at moments into tragedy, and perfectly absorbing to watch in its nature and development. She was a self-analyst in everything. Note the skill with which she lightly touches what she considers to be one of her characteristic defects: "I shall not be able to think of anything further I may wish to say till after the mail has gone. As you know, I am always obliged to call back the servants after they have got to the foot of the stairs." [24] But all the depth of penetration in the analytical instrument is chiefly applied to the dissection of these intensest of human relations, which she cannot understand, because nobody does, but which tantalize her, and perplex her, and fascinate her, in the ever-renewed effort to unravel them. The delicacy of this analysis will appear in nearly all the passages that I quote, but it cannot be better summed up than in the sentences in which she explains and defends the candor and directness of her letters: "I must express myself, and the varying feelings, and contending passions that beset me, and the look of men and of nature as seen through my eyes, or my letters will be so meager and threadbare you will not care to read them. It will not be me that writes, but a thing I am trying to fashion to suit you, which would soon become a nonentity, made up of platitudes. I will express the evil and the good that is in me, life as it looks to me, let my own individuality have fair expression (it will, no matter how close I hedge), and if I hurt sometimes, I may be able to atone at others." [25]

It is evident that, with such an analytical temperament, happiness, at least in this mingled world, is hardly possible. Nerves so constituted are exquisitely sensitive to joy, but they are too well aware that joy's hand is ever at his lips bidding farewell. Not that Mrs. Butler was a habitual and obvious pessimist. Far from it. Her husband asserts, "I never supposed you were a person who made a luxury of woe." [26] She was not. Nor did she generally complain or impose any unhappiness she had upon others: "No calamity will ever force me to make much outcry. I only know by the relief I feel how much I have been disturbed." [27] But the larger sense of human misery was never far off, and it takes little to make it well up in words

of strange, compelling beauty, sometimes merely
pathetic and appealing, sometimes with a note of
proud rebellion, almost of despair: "Oh, dear, I
shall die, with catching at straws. I could laugh
out like a maniac, but I won't. I have a great mind
to pack one trunk and go into Asia all by myself.
In that way, I might manage to stay in the world
by going out of it. Now, I am not good to-night,
nor resigned to what is placed before me, but I am
beset with an ugly feeling of humorous and fiendish
mockery at the way things look. No doubt some
evil thing is tampering with us. I will say my
prayers, put out the light, and creep into bed beside
of Blanche." [28]

These moods of restless distress were naturally
fostered and augmented by her husband's necessary
absence on his military duties. Sometimes she is
able to be in the South with him. But again he is
far, far away, and for all her cares and all her
intensely active occupations, she has too many minutes and hours when she dwells upon the remoteness
and the solitude and the hopeless, unforgetable
void. Though it is right and best for her not to be
with him for the time, she cannot reconcile herself
to it, longs unspeakably to tell him all she feels,
almost determines that they shall never be parted
again: "If that good time ever comes for us to meet,

we will return together, or stay away together. I will not come back alone. I am ready 'to tread the weary path' with you, wherever it leads, and can find no pleasure in any other. . . . I shall improve, believe me. The sad complaining that annoys will wear away." [29]

Above all, she not only wants to be with him, she wants him to want her with him, and the reiterated expression of this haunting lover's doubt and desire is strangely poignant in its intensity. Sometimes it appears in just a touch, part playful, part tender, part reproaching: "Well, dearest, would you like to see me? 'Yes, very well, if you did not weary me with asking the question!' Good night, good night." [30] Sometimes it develops in longer complaint, even with a suggestion of bitterness: "You may not be aware how much the tone of your letters has changed. In every letter I have asked, begged, to know if you wished me to come, and when. After telling me three times not to come, the only permission I have received is this: '*If* you can appear so and so I shall be glad to see you.' I shall be as God wills, and circumstances compel, subject to the same feelings as other people. But these are not reasons for or against seeing me, whether I am more or less merry. Be willing to make some effort on your own part to lift the weight that oppresses me, and see if I do not appreciate it. If life looks more inviting in that fair clime without me, say so; your letters have hurt me, I cannot bear it, nor the manner in which you have asked me to come." [31]

And immediately one wonders, how did the husband take all this, what was his attitude in the matter? It is suggested clearly enough in the sentences that gave rise to the above complaint: "Seriously, lovingly, with every kind thought, hope, and wish, I would be very happy; very, very pleased; very, very content; very, very much solaced to have you come *if* you are only happy, contented, pleased, solaced. I cannot endure to see you unhappy, that operates on me, and from its effect I make you more and more unhappy." [32] In short, it is the old, old story. He loves her with his whole heart, her love is an essential part of his life, perhaps the most essential part. But he is secure of it, and he is immensely busy with other interesting affairs. He really cannot be quite so preoccupied with sentiment, nor understand why she is. Again and again he expresses the tenderest, most obviously genuine feeling, not always with such words as hers, sometimes with his fatal lack of taste, but at other times very charmingly: "I have no thoughts of vexation at anything you write. If we live to meet again there will be no thought between us but of happi-

215

ness. I *know* and *feel it.* You have been in error in not showing your love. I have erred in not seeing it. . . . Be happy, dearest. Kiss the pillow for me, and believe the kiss that goes with this." [33]

When she is fretful and disturbed, he tries to laugh her out of it. Really, they have loved each other devotedly for twenty years, they are grown, middle-aged man and woman, above all they are in the thick of the world's great affairs, and is it not just a little trivial to let oneself be so tormented with the strange, subtle fancies of the heart? "What a pettish, mocking, sarcastic little thing it is? Railing at all the world, abusing the doctors, flying about, jumping out of its skin, and then boasting how 'calm and smooth' it is going to be. How it would like to have me by to torment me good every way." [34] Or, he takes things more seriously, begs that his already enormous cares should not be augmented by her who ought to relieve them: "Was ever a good, kind loving wife so afflicted with her own sad fancies? And your letter fell upon me like a stone." [35] Or, in a sadder, quieter mood, he feels that she has misunderstood him in her querulous criticism, but feels also the tender, moving charm of even her misunderstanding: "You make a part of the voyage of life on to its port of destination, that deviation which was and is but a stupid and

216

foolish blunder of the helmsman. You set down as a part of the original purpose and chart of the voyage acts which were only intended and done to correct the blunder of the steersman. But sadly, beautifully have you wrought it out, and admiration, love, sadness, pity, sympathy, and yearning tenderness, mingled with whirling celerity as I read. Ah me! That my faults should return to me with such vivid painting by such a hand." [30]

And is it not a study of strange fascination to see two persons, who were playing such a great and open part in the world, tearing away at each other's hearts, as if they were Antony and Cleopatra, and the world were indeed well lost for love? And she perfectly appreciates the strangeness, and admits it, and regrets it. She has been foolish, she has been mistaken, she will do differently. "How variable, how strange, you must think me! Yet I am not so. Only foolish that I cannot always forget myself. I know that what I should do is to cheer, and encourage. But if I could always do it, it would be so like a machine. It may be you would prefer to take me as I am. Fitful, wayward sometimes, but a very loving wife. . . . You have doubted this. You never need to doubt it more. Pride, that I once thought a ruling element, is subject and overborne by tenderness, sympathy, and other gentler feelings. Perhaps the first has passed away, and the others have grown stronger. Whatever it may be, I feel very tenderly toward you, and do not like to see you troubled." [37]

Yet she troubles him again, again intrudes the old, teasing, torturing doubts and wishes, till he actually rebels and speaks with a harshness that he does not mean any more than she means her complaint: "I knew too well the result, foresaw it, and was *fool* enough to be persuaded into changing what was a lifetime conviction upon some supposed idiocy that you were not like other women. Now you have a right to write me such admonitions, but you had better not." [38] And thus the old endless battle of the heart's unfulfilled desire is fought and will be, so long as the world endures. Only this woman portrays the battle with a singular clarity and force.

And it cannot be said that her distrust or distress ever go so far as actual jealousy, at least in her letters as printed for us. I have no reason to suppose that she had cause for such a feeling. Indeed, I am assured by an intimate friend of Mrs. Butler's, so far as such assurance goes, that she never had cause. On one occasion Butler attempts one of his peculiarly infelicitous jokes: "I must lose my housekeeper. . . . I shall have to get another.

What say you to a young, dashing, black-eyed bru-
nette, with a strong tongue and a sharp nose, that
will make us all stand around?" [39] And the suggestion is taken up in a manner that shows the far-off
sensitiveness of that clinging affection: "I see you
have not received my letters, or this matter of house-
keepers would not be presented either for blonds or
brunettes. But let that pass. Gilman can look that
the negroes do not destroy, there should be no other
servants in your house. I speak now for your own
honor, what might be supposed to affect me is of
little moment. None can make me less than I hold
myself, as *expecting* consideration, if I deserve
more it will be estimated hereafter." [40] Again the
anticipated presence of a young and pretty woman
causes a not unnatural twinge: "Mrs. Parton, too,
will have made the days lively while she is present.
But with all the pleasure that she or others have the
charm to give, you must yet 'remember to keep
promises, love.'" [41]

But such unhappiness as there is goes far deeper
than any temporary jealousy, strikes right down
to the fundamental incompatibilities and impossi-
bilities of separated human hearts. Always there
is that longing for perfect union and identity.
Always there is the hopelessness of achieving it.
Sometimes this is suggested in a brief, impersonal,

general touch: "Ah me! there is such a wide difference between man's thought and woman's." [42]
Sometimes it takes the form of a querulous petu-
lance, hardly intended or perhaps even realized:
"I verily believe my letters would be more welcome
to any man on your staff than they are to you,
and that is saying but little." [43] Sometimes there is
just the vast sense of fatigue and pettiness, the
vague desire to be caressed and cherished and
taken care of: "Oh, dearest, I feel just as Benny
does, when he creeps into my lap at night and wants
me to rock and sing to him. And there is nobody
to rock or sing or care anything about me. . . . I
especially wish to-night that somebody loved me, a
little, I am so tired; but I hardly think there is anyone can, it is so much work. And really it is folly
to trouble about it." [44] Or again, there is almost a
proud pleasure in superior sensibility, a feeling
that there is a distinction in the misery of analysis
itself, and that only those natures feel the separation and incompleteness which are really worthy to
be completed: "Life with people like you and me
cannot roll on like a long, calm, quiet summer's
day. We shall have the variety of the seasons,
storm, calm, the bright promise of spring, the sick
and melancholy glories of autumn. All experiences
of life will come to us because we are capable of

them all, we shall sound every string from the lowest note to the top of our compass. May we learn to touch those strings gently that produce discord." [45]

III

But everywhere and at all times, through all the analysis and all the suffering, the passion for identity is there, the desire to be lost in love itself, if not in the object of that love. The lover has no existence, desires none, except as she is bound up with the one being to whom she has relinquished all her fate. At least this is true for the period covered by the letters that are given to us. And the intensity of self-abandonment is made all the clearer by the slight glimpses we get of an earlier life, of more personal hopes and ambitions, which prevailed before love had conquered all. It is evident everywhere that ambition, the intense desire to realize one's full powers and do something great in the world, was inborn in this energetic spirit: "I see no indication in him, nor indeed in any that I meet, of superior talent, no lofty aspirations, no enthusiasm, no towering ambition that presses on in defiance of obstacles; though the development of these gifts is sometimes offensive in early youth to older people, they are the only incentives to noble actions, to future excellence." [46] Romance, the wide sweep of imagination, ever devising larger hopes and richer triumphs, was so native to her that neither years nor disappointments nor sorrows could wholly wear it away: "I do not live like other people, I am confident. I began life entirely different from those I knew. I am as far apart from them now as then. . . . In every fiber of me is woven a romance that will die when I am dead, and not till then. . . . It is not the school-girl fever, that must find an object, make a match, and then is commonplace forever. But a love of beauty, of art, even where it is not cultivated, an instinctive love of it in every form, in books, painting, poetry, and music. . . . There is a deep and keen sensibility in my nature that time does not deaden, I think it only intensifies." [47]

With this passionate attitude towards life, it is easy to conceive what it must have meant to abandon a career upon the stage, though no actual reference to this struggle is printed. The echo of it appears almost pathetically in the constant quotation of Shakespeare with which Mrs. Butler's letters are filled. It seems as if not only the better-known plays, but all of them, had become part of her thought and life to such an extent that bits from

them creep into her own writing almost unconsciously. And all this suggests that she might, at
some time, have had literary ambitions also. Certainly the power and beauty of her letters would
justify it, and I am convinced that if they could be
gathered in a volume by themselves, they would
gain a permanent place in American literature.

But whatever hopes of this kind she may have
cherished, it is obvious that they were gradually
lost and merged in the larger career of the brilliant, erratic personality to which she had attached
herself. From 1860 on, or probably from much
earlier, Mrs. Butler's ambition was her husband's
and her husband's only. As for the quality of his,
it undoubtedly lacked the pure, clear flame of hers;
but it was large and sweeping enough, some would
say, brutal enough, to absorb, if not to satisfy,
anyone. It was not lacking in the higher and finer
elements, either. Unquestionably there was a sincere motive of patriotism there, a desire and an
aspiration for the noblest things: "Whatever may
happen, I will leave a name my children will not
be ashamed to inherit, and a memory which will be
dear to a loved and loving wife." [48] But also, in
moments of enthusiasm, the ambition knew no
limits, reached out for the highest conception of
power, of course to be used for the highest good,

as in the notable passage: "It is coming—a 'Military Dictator.' God grant the man may be one of power and administrative capacity. Let it come —the man has not developed himself yet—but he will—in the field, too, before long. The day of small expedients and small men is getting by. Well, an empire is the repose as it is the ripeness of nations." [49]

Then, after the moods of enthusiasm, came the moods of discouragement. Merit was not recognized. Stupid cabals blighted honest effort. West Point hung like a cloud over real genius and intelligence and made advancement impossible. What was the use, anyway? With age creeping on, what was there left in life worth a man's ambition or his hope? "It is all a blank, and I think not of much consequence. There is not much worth living for to a man of forty-five. We have seen it all. How tame is life now in comparison with what it was! All's known. Why drag out a few more years to reiterate the same routine? Alas! for the enthusiasm of youth!" [50]

Yet right beside him all the time was this woman who never failed to stimulate, to encourage, to support. What does she answer to this complaint of insipidity? "I look upon your career as just begun. Never think you will not find pleasure in it. It is

only when hope is defeated for the time being that
one is indifferent. It springs again fresh as at first.
And every year the great game is played with increased interest (as it will be with you) till the
very aged are more reluctant to quit than the mere
youth." [51] What superb, unshakable confidence she
has in him. His intelligence, his will, his character
—who can equal them? "I do not often praise you,
but it is my firm belief that there is but *one man*
now known to the people who can save this country
in its present critical state from utter loss and confusion irremediable; and that is yourself. Not that
in time of peace and plenty you would be the best
or only man; but I have seen, nor heard of, no
man but you with broad and comprehensive views,
and also a determined will and grasp of power
(when within your reach) to carry them into
effect." [52] What a wife to have beside you, with
her arms and her heart about you!

And she did not stop with approval. She urged,
excited, spurred, to glorious deeds and great adventures. The stakes are high, immense; what matters
it, play on, play all: "There is but a step sometimes
between a crown and a gibbet, and in days like
these one cannot tell to which his labors will lead." [53]
Never falter, never flag! Fail? Screw your courage to the sticking-place, and you'll not fail. "You

225

have many times wrung triumph from the very clutch of despair, and will do it again and again, in despite of them all. Never yield an inch, or droop an hour, disheartened. It is the great game of life you are playing. And it goeth faster than a weaver's shuttle. Your brain spins swifter than other men, and you must *weave* while you *spin*." [54] And then she blends a dozen feelings and motives together—love, ambition, fidelity, Shakespearean reminiscence—and seasons it all with that sweet, subtle, tender marital playfulness which is both a cement of solidarity and a sad seal of separation: "So, so, I must not expect you here. You are so enamored with your trade, a day cannot be lost from it. You might exclaim with Antony, 'Oh, love, that you knew the royal occupation, then should you see a workman in it.' I shall not help to buckle on your armor, but I have mended your drawers and will return them to you when they are nicely pressed." [55]

And she not only stimulates generally, she understands and follows all the details of his thought and effort, and her advice and influence are evident at all stages of his career. Butler himself recognizes this amply: "Thus I had an advantage over most of my brother commanding generals in the department and in the field, in having an adviser faithful and true, clear-headed, conscientious, and conservative, whose conclusions could always be trusted. . . . All that she agreed to was right and for the best and if there is anything in my administration of affairs that may be questioned, it is that in which I followed the bent of my own opinions." [56]

Politics? There was not a quiver of his political aspiration which she did not understand and sympathize with. When she is at home in Lowell, she studies the situation carefully and analyzes its broader aspects in a way which she thinks impossible for him when engaged in actual combat. She implores him to cultivate some influences and to avoid others. Seward, much should be made of Seward. And she never ceases to deplore that she could not have had the opportunity of dealing with Seward herself. [57] Grant, Lincoln, all of them must be handled with care and tact. So must the people at large, and if they are, surely in the end they must come to appreciate the absolute necessity of falling back upon her idol for salvation. "Kimball I think is a Lincoln man. Now, can you tell me why this thing is so? Why won't they choose you? Almost the only man who has really accomplished anything in this war! The only one in the party who, at the head of Government, can carry it to a successful issue." [58]

But interested and interesting as Mrs. Butler is in politics, she is even more so in military matters. The plumed troop and the big wars are not remote from her, far from it. She studies all her husband's military associates and has her most distinct opinion about them. This one is a help and a resource, to be relied on and trusted. That other will fail at a pinch; do not believe in him, keep away from him. Above all, she is urgent against unnecessary friction. She knows well his forthright, violent ways, and what a danger they involve: "You must not have further trouble with the army officers,— if the provocation is ever so bitter, if it is possible to avoid it. They can strike the heaviest, for they strike in a body." [59] She follows actual movements in the field with passionate solicitude, and drives home her injunctions with sledge-hammer vigor: "*Think,* while you have the time, note everything great and small, trace back every step of this campaign, see if there has been a blunder made, and what is likely to be Grant's movement from this time out, and where you would be able to strike the best blow if they send you more troops." [60]

Oh, that she were a man. Not that she is really unwomanly, unfeminine, or gives that impression;

228

she does not. She is keenly susceptible of fear, and admits it, fear on occasion for herself, much more the wife's and lover's fear for him. Repeatedly she begs him not to expose himself foolishly or unnecessarily. But when the tense strain comes, when her eager fancy is kindled by ambition and love, then all the woman is melted out of her and she is ready for any high emprise: "The death of General Williams has nerved me like steel. Would I were a man. I am stronger in the hour of danger, for then I forget myself and woman's cares, and feel all the high enthusiasm that leads to deeds of fame, and for this reason it is better that I should be with you. I could never pull you back from what I thought it your duty to do, but should urge you forward, and help, with all the wit I have." [61] The concrete instance of this splendid urgency that touches me most is Butler's own account of his wife's conduct when the troop-ship which he commanded was stranded and in imminent danger off Cape Hatteras. Mrs. Butler tells the story vividly, but makes little of her part in it. Her husband depicts his discouragement and almost despair. With no subordinates on whom he could rely, with slight marine experience of his own, he was almost ready to give up hope and even control. "As I sat with my hand covering my face, I felt a light touch on my shoulder. I looked up and Mrs. Butler was standing beside me. 'Cheer up,' she was saying; 'do the best you can, resume your command, and perhaps all will be well.' " [62] All was well, and the woman's quiet words carried him through that crisis, as they carried him through so much of life.

Not that at all times she was not keenly aware of his weaknesses and deficiencies. These wives, with their terrible vision, always are aware. Sometimes she cautions, sometimes she chides, sometimes she mocks gently: "So, so, 'sufferance is the badge of all your tribe,' is it? You make me smile. It is the one quality you most heartily abjure,—patience and sufferance will never be guests of yours. If pressed in they will get cheap entertainment and speedily be shown the door." [63] But let anyone else criticize, and how quickly she leaps to his defense. His enemies get no consideration, no comfort, no support from her. They are animated by prejudice and mean envy, and in the end the sure old arbiter, time, will bring their devices to naught.

It is perhaps here that we should observe just the slightest trace in her of that lack of a higher, finer delicacy which is so deplorably obvious in him. Not that we are to infer it in her because she loved him; alas! we see the love of higher, finer natures just so erring every day. But at times she

230

has a touch of his acerbity which I regret. Also, I could wish that she had stood out resolutely against the gifts which he was constantly sending from the South to her and to others. Of one such case she writes: "Mr. Butler has sent his mother a service of silver, four pieces, he bought it by weight. There has been so much talk, I would not say much about it if I were her, for envy makes people bitter. . . . There is nothing to conceal, but envious minds will not believe so." [64] There may have been nothing to conceal, but at least such purchases were wrung from the cruel necessity of war, and it was far better to eschew them altogether, as Sherman did.

Yet these minor matters must not for a moment be understood to imply any essential flaw in the nobleness of the woman's spirit. She aimed high always, looked high, loved high, in a lofty fashion and for lofty purposes. However her beloved might strive highly, she wished him to strive holily. Just how much she knew about the complicated business transactions that went on under Butler's administration we cannot tell, because we know too little about them ourselves. But we do know that wherever he went, he was followed by a train of financial adventurers, always ready to make commercial advantage out of the necessities of friend and enemy alike, and that this train brought upon his reputation a cloud of discredit such as affects no other commander of equal rank, either North or South. And at least it is evident that the wife knew enough about it all to feel the intense danger and scandal of it, to understand that he was wantonly and foolishly imperiling his happiness and hers, and all the larger, saner ambition which she so deeply cherished for him.

With what profound, keen insight does she analyze, even at an early stage, the weakness which held so much possibility of evil: "Beside the fond devotion of a wife, there is still the same responsibility felt by me for whatever you may do, as there was years ago when you laid your head on my lap, and prayed me to look kindly and lovingly into your face. I saw then what I have since seen in Paul, but not in the other children, peculiarities easily wrought upon, and dangerous from their very simplicity. . . . Yes, and that readiness to believe in the *"fair outward seeming"* is but an indication of your faith in deeper, higher, and holier objects, though these you may often turn away from and seem to disregard. Guard against this last, oh, dear love, guard against it. Try not ever with sophistries to obscure to your own mind the clear dividing lines of right and wrong." [65] How tersely and how ardently does she caution him

232

against the tendencies that beset him: "No man that I brought into the Department, were I you, should be allowed to do things that I did not fully understand." [66] Again, "Keep the men whom you know to be honorable, capable business men, who are decent in their morals and conduct, and root out the others without mercy." [67] With what a cry of distress does she deplore the influence of those who, she sees too clearly, are working ruin and disaster: "Is it not enough to make one mad that [after] two years of agony which I have borne, and after I had proved to him that Jackson was the cause of his failure at Fortress Monroe, yet again that he should bestow all power and give all confidence once more, to have his reputation assailed, and the power he has and might yet gain, slip from his grasp and crumble to nothing?" [68]

Yet through it all not for one moment does the love falter or the devotion fail. She has merged her heart and her hope and her life in this love, and neither heaven nor hell nor eternity can shake it. All that she has and is and can be depends upon the desperate effort for identity with this other soul which, as all souls do, eludes her grasp and flits away from her. For still, still, back of the effort for identity is the everlasting impossibility of it, which makes the tragedy of marriage, the tragedy of love, the tragedy of all our baffled, frail, uncertain human life. As Matthew Arnold has it, our souls are petty islets, set forever apart in an impassable, unfathomable ocean.

Yes, in the sea of life enisled
     .   .   .   .   .
We mortal millions live *alone.*
     .   .   .   .   .

But when the moon their hollows lights,
And they are swept by balms of spring,
And in their glens on starry nights,
The nightingales divinely sing,
     .   .   .   .   .

Oh, then a longing like despair
Is to their farthest caverns sent,
For surely once, they feel, they were
Parts of a single continent.
     .   .   .   .   .

A god, a god their severance ruled,
And bade betwixt their shores to be
The unplumbed, salt, estranging sea.

VIII

MRS. JAMES GILLESPIE BLAINE

CHRONOLOGY

Harriet Stanwood Blaine.
Born, Augusta, Maine, October 12, 1828.
Married James Gillespie Blaine, 1850.
Blaine, Secretary of State, 1881.
Blaine, nominated for the Presidency, 1884.
Blaine, Secretary of State, 1889-1892.
Blaine died, January 27, 1893.
Died, July 15, 1903.

MRS. JAMES GILLESPIE BLAINE

I

TAKING his whole career together, James G. Blaine was perhaps the man who came nearest to the Presidency without getting it, and the excitement and the struggle, as well as all the variegated passion of his long life, are reflected in the heart and in the letters of Harriet Stanwood Blaine.

Mrs. Blaine was born at Augusta, Maine, in 1828, two years before her distinguished husband. She was educated in Augusta and in Ipswich, Massachusetts. She then went to teach in Kentucky, and there met Blaine and married him in 1850. From that time on her life was identified with his, and she entered passionately into all his experiences, as Speaker of the Maine House of Representatives, of the national House, as candidate for the presidential nomination in 1876, 1880, and 1892, for the Presidency in 1884, and in his different terms of service as Secretary of State. She presided over various extensive establishments, brought up a large family of sons and daughters, and alto-

237

gether led a most varied and brilliant life till the
death of her two elder sons and a daughter shortly
preceded that of their father in 1893. Her remaining years were darkened by sorrow and affliction,
and she died in a pitiful state of mind and body.

Practically all of Mrs. Blaine's married life was
passed in intimate contact with the great world and
with the most wide and striking contrasts of humanity. Her husband had a vast acquaintance and
the reflection of it naturally came to her. She met
men of business and men of pleasure, scholars, soldiers, artists, and hundreds of politicians, and the
wives of many of them. In Europe she saw royalty,
and met it as serenely as she did presidents and
shoeblacks. Humanity was humanity to her; the
garb made little difference.

On the whole, she liked and enjoyed it. She was
curious about the lives of people, interested in their
fortunes and especially in their motives. She says
of her son, "He writes me nice long letters, giving
me details which I dearly love." [1] So did Madam
de Sévigné. In Europe she goes dutifully and in-
dustriously to see sights, but remarks with a slight
yawn of boredom, "There is nothing in ruins or
any other dead or going things comparable to the
interest of living people and homes." [2]

She had a profound and persistent instinct for

observation and analysis, and was always ready and quick with shrewd comment on the doings and sayings of the men and women about her. But it is notable that, for all their shrewdness, her comments are not usually harsh or bitter, but incline to be tempered with sympathy and understanding and the gift of entering into others' lives. She had indeed a singular frankness, a candor of tongue and pen that is sometimes startling. Also she had a sweet and gracious irony which plays over all sorts of subjects and experiences, slight or serious, and which gives her letters an extraordinary charm. She has not the imaginative depth or power of Sarah Butler, but she has much more ease and natural grace of expression in all connections. I have sometimes wondered whether she had any thought that her letters would one day be published. She cites Mrs. Carlyle, whose correspondence she enjoyed intensely, as evidence that "letters do survive and that the public reads." [3] But if she had any such consciousness, it did not mar in the slightest the spontaneous flow of her comment on herself and the world.

The instinct for acute observation is with her at all times and leads to subtle tracing of humanity in the midst of great scenes and events. Take her significant hint of what went on at the White House

in the tragic days after Garfield's assassination:
"I am afraid to trust things to pen and ink. Character comes out so surprisingly at such times, and
many of the ladies who are around manage to have
such a good time." [4] Take again her brief and vivid
portrayal of all sorts of people. It may be the
furnace-man at Augusta. It may be the British
ambassador. Always she depicts him as he is, or as
he appears to her, with unshrinking veracity. Sometimes it is a touch of serious and profound emotion,
as in the description of a friend, "he impresses
you all the time as on the thither side of life and
conscious of it." [5] Sometimes it is a lighter and
more sarcastic turn about some one perfectly insignificant: "Mrs. Wood . . . kept me waiting a
long time, and then was full of apologies about
her dress; from which I infer that mothers are the
same in palace and hovel." [6] Or, for a more elaborate study, take the portrait of President Arthur,
whom, to be sure, Mrs. Blaine had personal reasons
for not loving; but you feel that you have the man,
all the same: "I do not think he knows anything.
He can quote a verse of poetry or a page from
Dickens and Thackeray, but these are only leaves
springing from a root out of dry ground. His
vital forces are not fed, and very soon he has given
out his all. . . . The last time he was here, he spoke

to me of his chagrin that we had not been invited
to the White House, but time wears on, and the
invitation lingers, and I do not think a perfectly
well-bred President would make such an apology.
He certainly commands his own house and table. I
hear in society only approving words. Can a President be otherwise than fascinating, pleasant, intelligent, and delightfully welcome?" [7]

It is to be observed that Mrs. Blaine's human
interest was mainly social, not philanthropic. There
is plenty of evidence that she was sensitive to individual unhappiness and suffering. Again and again
little hints slip in of the doing of kindly and
thoughtful things and of little sacrifices made,
though any ostentation would have been perfectly
abhorrent to her. Her passionate sympathy with
the Garfield sufferers is as clearly sincere as it is
simple in statement: "He . . . beckoned, and when
I went to him, pulled me down, kissed me again
and again, and said, 'Don't leave me until Crete
comes.' I took my old bonnet off and just stayed.
I never left him a moment. Whatever happened
in the room, I never blenched, and the day will
never pass from my memory." [8] But she does not
seem to have much burdened herself with elaborate
philanthropy, and "causes" and "reforms" do not

241

appear in her pages, for which I at least am grateful.

It is of interest to determine how far, in this wide contact with humanity, Mrs. Blaine made herself acceptable and popular with people in general; but there is some conflict of opinion. It is evident that she was not universally liked and the reasons are easy to understand. She was a person of strong, quick feelings, readily hardening into prejudice. Her subtle and keen insight was swift to penetrate pretense and sham of every kind, and her extraordinarily frank, direct tongue conveyed her judgments with remarkable energy and effect. In a world so built of conventions as that of general society, mere frankness, although without harshness or bitterness, is enough to inspire dread and mistrust. Even the sympathetic biographer speaks of "the pungency of phrase which . . . caused some injury to her own popularity." [9]

On the other hand, it is clear that when Mrs. Blaine liked her company, she could be extremely attractive. She had a noble and dignified presence, was tall in stature and stately in movement. She had excellent taste in dress, and without the slightest tendency to display, took care to see that she was always suitably appareled. Her own delicate mockery in this matter, as in all, is delightful. "I

have collected and had colored black, all the stray
feathers in the house; and you ought to see my hat
which they adorn. . . . It is as big as the moon
after the eclipse had passed off the other night,
and all around the edge of this great orb, these
plumes arise, solemnly rustling in the west wind
which has now been blowing for lo, these many
days. . . . Nothing could be prettier than it looks
on Alice — of it on myself modesty forbids me
to speak." [10] Her conversation was as brilliant and
sparkling as her letters, and those with whom she
was really intimate must have found her a perpetual source of instruction and entertainment. As
to social tact, she probably had plenty of it when
she cared to use it. Her own opinion of her gifts
in this line was perhaps somewhat higher than
that of others. In regard to an irksome invitation
she says: "I have peremptory orders from headquarters to decline, which I have done in honeyed
accents, very different from those in which the lion
refused to be bored." [11]

That the pressure of humanity should sometimes
be too much for her was natural. When she was
worn and tired, she felt that she never wished to
enter a drawing-room again, or to have anybody
enter hers. In expressing the incapacity of weary

nerves to meet the demands, she gets a touch of Emily Dickinson's fiery brevity: "Altogether, if I had felt strong, I would have enjoyed it, but it seems to me I am asked to fill immensity with my presence, and I cannot do it." [12] Yet there can be no doubt of her general enjoyment of the life she was called upon to live. She had her moments of relishing solitude, of longing to get out of the bustle into some region of quiet thought. But the moments were few and they did not last. The habit of wide and constant movement grew upon her, and as long as she had strength and happiness, she found herself mainly at home in it. "I can give you no idea of the bustle we live in. Our small rooms, irregular habits, Tom always in the parlor, the cards, the notes, the letters which cumber every table, the great crowd of personal friends of your father in Washington, all of whom desire to see him, and their wish should be gratified." [13] It was all pleasant and welcome, and a person with eyes and ears and a heart and a brain like hers could not fail to find such vast human opportunities both entertaining and profitable.

II

Now let us narrow the circle of observation and see Mrs. Blaine in her home and domestic surroundings. Her letters give the same quiet and delightful play of irony about these as about the larger world.

Here I may perhaps mention that in preparing this portrait I have resorted to methods of personal investigation which I have rarely used before to such an extent. There is no formal biography of Mrs. Blaine. On the other hand, there are many persons living who remember her well. Therefore I sent out a table of questions to a number of these persons, hoping to get information which would be a valuable supplement to the letters. My inquiries were answered with the utmost cordiality and courtesy by everyone, and I have only gratitude for this sympathetic response. At the same time, I do not think I shall again try the experiment. I got more information than I wanted. That is to say, the replies were too general to have any vivid significance, and on the other hand they were altogether too contradictory. Mrs. Blaine was delightful to meet. She was very unpopular. She was without ambition, social or otherwise. She was intensely ambitious. She was in the highest degree helpful to Mr. Blaine. She was exceedingly damaging. She was an excellent housekeeper. She was no housekeeper at all. No doubt the satanic ingenuity of the practiced biographer can reduce all these conflicts to a halting sort of harmony. But I feel safer in relying upon the evidence of the letters, unimpeachable so far as it goes, in regard to domestic interests and everything else.

During the greater part of her married life Mrs. Blaine lived in comfort and luxury. She had a full realization of this and often portrays or suggests it charmingly: "I am left absolutely alone with my servants, every want anticipated, not a room in the house not at summer heat, sunshine and open fires vying with each other, four horses and pony in the stable, sleighs and robes in abundance and the beautiful snow; every longing satisfied, with full salvation blessed—what can I need?" [14] Yet all this comfort could not be achieved and maintained without care. There were vast responsibilities upon her always, and whether she discharged them well or ill, and I feel sure it was in the main well, she could not get rid of them, and she sometimes sighed over them. There were establishments in Washington, establishments in Augusta, establishments in Bar Harbor. There were guests coming and going. There were husband and children who did not go, or went when you least counted upon it. "This is one of my tavern weeks — the board being spread for all who come," she says. [15] And when she is older and has kept it up for years, she murmurs: "I am so tired that one kitchen with myself for cook and no dining room attached would look as enviable as Naboth's vineyard." [16]

Servants were a luxury, but they were a trouble when you were the one to manage them. There is the best of evidence that she was kind and considerate with those who worked for her, and her own words indicate it often. Even when she found the work ill done and the workers trying, there is a note of human kindness in her complaint: "What it will be to me to get rid of this loyal, unfaithful servant! Everything about the place is going to waste, and it becomes each season more difficult to obtain tidiness or neatness, much less nicety, in carriage, horse, or garden. My very soul is tired, trying to get the wood for an open fire sawed and cut. The fires are always mighty conflagrations or beds of ashes." [17]

Also, to have servants, you have to have money, and money was one of the greatest cares and responsibilities to Mrs. Blaine, as to the rest of us. The resources were usually sufficient, often ample, but they were uncertain. Blaine's salary, when he had it, was considerable, and at all times he had an active and on the whole shrewd business instinct. But he had a decided taste for expenditure and also for speculation, and his doings in this way were

apt to be hazardous and were not always creditable.
In any case, they worried his wife, who was of a
more provident and cautious disposition, though
the gleam of gentle mockery appears even here: "I
am about my dressmaking, and my dearer self—
and certainly he might apply the title with another
significance to me—is looking up his sadly neglected
stocks. The only question now is, are they worth
taking any notice of? All that fine Fortunatus's
purse which we once held the strings of, and in
which we had only to insert the finger to pay there-
with for the house, has melted from the grasp which
too carelessly held it, and we must look about for
new investments, the comfort of which I find is the
inference that there is still enough left to spare for
investments." [18]

And the uncertainty of income made spending,
always so deplorably certain, an anxious matter to a
careful housekeeper. She saves and clips and cur-
tails where she can; but the needs are great, children must be clothed, visitors must be fed, a suitable
appearance in the world must be kept up, the bills
rain in, and sometimes she cannot imagine which
way to turn, though here also she smiles rather than
weeps. "Any difficulty but that of money I could
perhaps surmount, but the unknown, and money is
always to me the unknown factor, frightens me." [19]

Even an almost empty purse is matter for a sort of tender raillery: "I hovered on the outskirts to bid him good-bye, afraid to come recklessly to the front lest he should want some money, and I have only three silver quarters in my dear little purse, that cunning leather pouch which Jamie gave me." [20]

One of the husband's costly tastes was an especial cause of anxiety and trouble, though also of varied interest, his passion for building houses. The letters have many references to the picking out of lots, and weighing of their comparative merits, the attraction of views, the varied possibilities of construction, and the expense of it all. Then when the house was finished, it had to be furnished, and the housekeeper had to pick and choose, and arrange, and last and worst, to pay. And she had to dismantle, as well as to mantle, and the dismantling is a cheerless business which these merry designers of houses are apt to shirk: "I am waiting now only to be strong backed and clear headed to tear this house to pieces, and by this time next Sunday, I doubt not to see these beautiful portières and curtains rolled away like a scroll, these carpets transplanted like Aladdin's, no *man* knows whither, only one woman, in short, everything that moth and dust can corrupt withdrawn from the world." [21]

Whatever question there may be as to Mrs. Blaine's capability in other departments of housekeeping, there seems to be none as to her table. She takes a constant interest in the subject, both as affects her own household and that of others. When Garfield is ill, she complains bitterly of the White House cuisine: "Such tough leather as they had there for breakfast the other morning is a disgrace to the cattle on a thousand hills." [22] And Garfield's own comment is perhaps the greatest compliment to her, "When I am ready to eat, I am going to break into Mrs. Blaine's larder." [23] It is evident that she knew what good food was, knew its importance in domestic happiness and social success, and meant to have it available in her house at all times and under all circumstances.

As to family affairs in the Blaine household we have as abundant and as interesting testimony as with material conditions. Mrs. Blaine had many more or less distant relatives, and while it is clear that she did not care for all of them, she speaks of some with tenderness and appreciation. Perhaps the nearest was Miss Abigail Dodge (Gail Hamilton), Blaine's biographer, who was a frequent inmate. A certain amount of friction between two such high-strung and sensitive women was to be expected; but Miss Dodge was often of the greatest

usefulness and some of Mrs. Blaine's most brilliant
letters are addressed to her.

With her children Mrs. Blaine is charming. She
toiled over them in every way, from the humblest
mending of their garments to the most elaborate
thought for their intellectual and spiritual welfare.
When they are ill, she cares for them, and when
they are well, she enjoys them. When they are with
her, she makes them happy, and when they are
absent she writes them letters of clinging, longing
tenderness, as well as of delightful vivacity. How
sweet is her comment on her tendency to indulgence: "He is so kind and pleasant and so bright
and gay that I can refuse him nothing; I make a
very poor mother." [24] But her indulgence was not
extravagant. She knew how to reprove, if not to
chide, and it is said that most of the family discipline fell to her, since the father was so much away
from home. Yet, in spite of this, the children, who
adored their father, adored their mother also. How
could they help it? She took such endless pride
in them, and such endless comfort: "Then the boys
—oh, how I miss them. They know all I ever knew
—and I have forgotten much—they are fresh and
untiring as the sun which never sets—they are
loving and want sympathy—old enough to be com-
panions, too young to assert their rights, taking

everything as of grace, and of their fullness I am a partaker. Blessed relationship—the man child to his mother." [25]

So we see that, in her home surroundings, as in her contact with the more external world, Mrs. Blaine lived an intensely crowded and active life. She was rushed from one call to another, from one need to another, till it seemed as if no minute were left even for essential repose: "The one luxury which I cannot command is time: it may be made for slaves, but it is the breath of life to free men." [26] Yet it might be worth while to give all one's time and more to win from a daughter such beautiful and touching words as these: "She who never gave a thought to herself, living only in the lives of others, who was content to be used, absorbed, obliterated if need be, in her service of love, lives once more in these rescued leaves, in her forcefulness, her honesty, her humor, and her splendid courage that was so cruelly tried." [27]

III

Again, let us narrow the circle and take Mrs. Blaine's relation to her husband, so engrossing, so absorbing, that it almost seems as if the other relations did not exist. Her social life, her general domestic life, active and busy as they were, centered in the end on him. Even her children, much as she loved them, were disregarded when their father's interests were imperiled: "What are you, my dearest boy, what care I for any other name than your father's?" [28]

And still there is the play of light irony, about the one great love, as about everything else, of irony mingled with tenderness in a quaint fusion which is always delightful. She adores the man, but she sees his weaknesses, and in her confidential letters to her children she trifles with the weaknesses, oh, so gently.

Now as to clothes, his taste in clothes, or his mighty indifference to them, is curious, to a woman's eye. Cleanliness he cares for, but appropriateness he utterly disregards. When a sudden occasion presses, garments have to be hunted up from everywhere, disconnected things gathered together, and contributions levied on everyone. Old clothes? Why should any one complain of them? You know what they are like and how they have served you: "When I went down into the parlor on my way to the sleigh, I found all the burners lighted, while he turned himself about and about, admiring old clothes as good as new—*as* good! a thousand times better in his eyes." [29] What wife is there who will not understand?

Then his regularity, or lack of it. One may not be always exact oneself, but when one is trying to keep a perfect household, it is a little vexatious to have the chief figure in it so uncertain as to the time element and to what appear to be the first principles of order. Nor is the vexation greatly diminished by the knowledge that when the necessities of business require it, he can be as precise as any one. Note the delicious blend of feelings in the following: "First of all, I miss Mr. Blaine. I cannot bear the orderly array of my life. I miss the envelopes in the gravy, the bespattered table linen, the uncertainty of the meals, for you know he always starts out on his constitutional when he hears them taking in dinner." [30] And another passage is a trifle more serious, yet not too serious. Speaking of her eldest son, she says: "He . . . stood between me and all anxiety in a way which your father, dear and interesting as he has always been, never knew how to do." [31]

We have already seen what were the anxieties and difficulties about money. Mrs. Blaine does not attribute to herself any great gift at economy. She liked pleasant and costly things, and was not the one to blame indulgence in them. Her reference to her husband's "dearer self" shows that she did not claim entire immunity from these weaknesses.

But dollars had been scarce in her youth and in her later life she could not quite get used to the free, uncertain flow of them: "If anyone had told me at your age, Jamie, that I should ever have $20,000 to handle at my own sweet will, I should have believed in him or her, just as I believed in Aladdin's lamp, fascinating but supernatural." [32] A reckless and especially a careless expenditure worried her. Horses were agreeable, houses were agreeable; but where was the cash to come from? When you had to pay the bills, and the burden of adjustment and settlement came upon you, there were moments of worry, even approaching impatience: "I have drawn so much money this month, how can anyone who never listens to or enters into a detail, understand it?" [33]

Particularly interesting is Mrs. Blaine's constant comment on her husband's health. He was naturally vigorous, but he was sensitive and imaginative. How deftly does the wife suggest the alternations of a nervous temperament in her brief picture of the morning hours: " 'Oh, mother, mother Blaine,' he said, 'I have so much to do, I know not which way to turn.' 'Good!' said I. 'Yes,' said he, 'isn't it perfectly splendid?' A very different cry from the, 'Oh, mother, mother Blaine, tell me what is the matter with me!' which has so often assailed my earliest waking ear, and which always makes my very soul die within me." [34] As years went on, he become more and more solicitous as to what was the matter with him. Not only his wife, but his sons and his biographer bear witness to his excessive fondness for doses and doctors. And the wife ministers to him, evidently with watchful care and perfect tenderness. When real maladies assailed, as they often did, no one could be more devoted than she. But she had an active and strenuous soul, and the perpetual nursing of the chimney corner sometimes fretted even her, since she felt that he might forget himself and be making over the world. When the great decision as to a possible presidential candidacy in 1888 had to be made, she grew a little restless about it: "This is one of the days when I am not in sympathy with disease, when it seems to me that your father is in full possession of all his powers, eating and sleeping well, driving, alert in mind, memory . . . undimmed. . . . And with these prodigious powers the chimney corner and speculation on his own physical condition are all that he allows himself. A pity!" [35]

Nor is the irony entirely lacking even in her discussion of the affectionate relation between them. He loves her, oh yes, she knows how he loves her. Also, the great world needs him, and she is proud

of it, and would not have him lay aside his important duties for a moment for any little need of
hers. Yet there are hours when she is sick and weak
and lonely, and she would like him beside her, if it
were possible. As it is not, the best way is to smile
about it. "I could hardly let him go, I needed his
reviving society so much. . . . He had to go, but
felt that my desire to keep him was all right and
natural, so, with a man's appreciation of a woman's
nature, he promised to buy silk dresses for M. and
Alice, to say nothing of half a dozen for myself." [36]
Then she sums up the lovely mixture of his great
duties and his domestic feelings in a phrase which
many wives will thoroughly enjoy: "I miss his un-
varying attention and as constant neglect." [37] All
which is not to be understood as for a moment implying that Blaine was an indifferent husband.
On the contrary, he was a most affectionate one,
and his wife knew it well. There is the strongest
evidence that he was peculiarly devoted to his family, as appears in his charming remark, when some
one wondered how he could write with all his children about him, "It is because they *are* here that I
can write," [38] and in the comment of his biographer
on his fireside, "which he believed, and pronounced,
and made the happiest fireside in the world." [39]

As to Mrs. Blaine's fundamental devotion to him,

particular evidence is hardly necessary, since it is written on almost every page of her letters. To be sure, the many letters which she must have written to him no longer exist. She took care that they should disappear, hunting them out when he returned from any absence and destroying them herself. Only one or two escaped this searching effort on her part. In these the restraint and dignity of her tone are noticeable, as well as its surpassing tenderness and sweetness. But for all the restraint, it is clear that she gave her whole heart and her whole life in the hasty love match that took place in those early Kentucky years. They may have married in haste, but they never found a moment's leisure to repent, and the marriage continued to be a love match to the end. Her words to others on the subject are necessarily slight and brief, but they are enough to indicate how complete and absorbing the affection was and how permanent was its hold upon her.

With such a nature as hers, and his, and with such a long and deep love established between them, it is evident that her influence must have counted vastly in all the doings of his life. Just how did it count, is the question. Was she a help or a hindrance to his political career, and how much? She frequently expresses a dislike for politics in the abstract! "Sometimes I am so deeply disgusted with American politics, our whole system of popular government, with its fever, its passion, excitement, disappointment, and bitter reaction, that any sphere, however humble, which gives a man to his family, seems to me better than the prize of high place." [40] But he who was the main substance of her life was so constantly interested in them, that she could not keep her thoughts off them, and her temper was so ardent that, if she thought of them at all, she must think eagerly, must help, advise, remonstrate. "Your father and I have picked out Garfield's Cabinet for him, and have devoted to him for two mornings our waking, but not risen, hours." [41] That is the note that often recurs.

As to the effect of this active interest on Blaine's fortunes opinions differ remarkably. I am assured by some persons that she was a great help to him. Others assert that her influence was disastrous and almost fatal. This view is perhaps most forcibly stated by Peck, in connection with Mrs. Blaine's antipathy to Mrs. Harrison, and consequent persuasion of her husband to retire from Harrison's Cabinet and let his name be used in 1892 as an opposition candidate. "It was, in truth, upon Mrs. Blaine that the responsibility of this rather pitiable *dénouement* rested. No authorized explanation of

Mr. Blaine's sudden retirement from the Cabinet
has ever been put forth, yet it was perfectly well
known to many at the time that this step, so ill-
advised and so contrary to Mr. Blaine's own judgment, was taken because of his wife's insistence.
Mrs. Blaine was a very masterful, high-spirited
woman, unblessed with tact and far too prone to
interfere with her husband's political concerns.
More than once in his career this interference had
caused him great embarrassment." [42]

There may be much truth in this. At the same
time, I feel that while certain elements of injury in
Mrs. Blaine's influence may have been more obvious
and spectacular, the elements of helpfulness must
have been more constant and more important. To
have that clear, shrewd, analytical intelligence
thoughtfully working at all times on political events
and characters was of incalculable benefit to a man
so impulsive and so sensitive as Blaine, ever apt
to be unduly confident and unduly depressed. The
evidence of this is scattered all through Mrs.
Blaine's letters. It appears also in repeated testimony of Blaine himself, perhaps most suggestively
in the word to Garfield, "I want you to read my
letters to Mrs. Garfield . . . the advice of a sensible woman in matters of statecraft is invalu-
able." [43] The most charming touch of all in regard

to it is Mrs. Blaine's tender comment, "He's all right, but he loves the confessional and the lay sister (me) — why, I do not know, as I always shrive him out of hand," [44]

Whatever may be thought of the value of Mrs. Blaine's advice, there can be no question as to her immense admiration of her husband's powers and achievement. Oh, she could criticize in all ways, of course: it was her nature to do so. But her passionate devotion and esteem far outwent the criticism and altogether buried it. She admired him socially, felt as keenly as anyone that singular charm which is insisted upon by so many, but by none with more succinct grace than by her: "Your father being in one of his irresistible moods, when no man, I care not who he may be, can surpass him. Then, as Mr. Chandler says, I would rather hear him than eat." [45] She believed in his ability, believed in his simplicity, his sincerity, found in him all the essential elements of greatness: "You cannot imagine how grand your father seems to me; perfectly simple and natural, sleeping well and eating, and without one particle of pettiness or vanity in his whole composition." [46] Above all, when he was attacked and vilified, the fiery energy of her spirit rushed to his defense. Could any wife say more than she says, in the fierce hours of the

Fisher scandal and the Mulligan letters? "I dare to say that he is the best man I have ever known. Do not misunderstand me, I do not say that he is the best man that ever lived, but that of the men whom I have thoroughly known, he is the best." [47] Could the interplay of qualifying analysis and passionate affection be better illustrated than in that? The more one ponders on the sentence, the more one is impressed by the rich significance of it.

And as she admired him and loved him, so she entered into every phase and every aspect of his varying career with intense and enthusiastic sympathy. In the events that were more external to him, like the Garfield assassination and the excitement which ensued, she showed keen and anxious ardor of interest. And the ardor was even greater in what directly affected her husband himself. His Speakership, his Secretaryship, his chances for nomination in 1876, 1880, 1888, and 1892, all are the subjects of her constant comment, as eagerly sympathetic as it is lucid. But the zeal with which she followed his fortunes appears most in her description of the crisis of the great campaign of 1884, in which Blaine and all his friends had reckoned securely upon success. I do not know where you will find a more agonizing account of political suspense and final defeat than in that speaking page: "I was absolutely certain of the election as I had a right to be from Mr. Elkins's assertions. Then the fluctuations were so trying to the nerves. It is easy to bear now, but the click-click of the telegraph, the shouting through the telephone in response to its never-to-be-satisfied demand, and the unceasing murmur of men's voices, coming up through the night to my room, will never go out of my memory—while over and above all, the perspiration and chills, into which the conflicting reports constantly threw the physical part of one, body and soul alike rebelling against the restraints of nature, made an experience not to be voluntarily recalled." [48] Madame de Sévigné's great narratives can hardly beat that.

IV

With yet one more contraction of the circle, let us consider Mrs. Blaine's inmost world, that of her own closest thoughts and her own soul. In spite of all her devotion to her husband, of all her immense, intense outward activity, I feel that she kept this inner world apart and intact, more, for instance, than Sarah Butler did, though perhaps if we had Mrs. Blaine's letters to her husband, as we have Mrs. Butler's, the impression would be different. It was not so much any distinct intellectual or æsthetic enthusiasm; it is simply a sense in her of a certain self-poise and self-possession, clung to instinctively, unconsciously, yet always with an unfailing vigor of freedom.

If we knew more of her early life, perhaps we could trace more of the foundations of this strong individuality. But little is told us. It is probable that a nature so intense must have had quick, strong impulses in youth, and have required years to get control of them. She gives us slight charming glimpses of those early days, as in the account of a fit of homesickness at nine years old.[49] She was passionately fond of study, she says,[50] and the results of it show in the bits of Latin scattered over her pages, as in many other things. She regrets that she did not make better use of her opportunities: "If I could only have known, when your age, the high plane on which I should deploy, I might have been the equal in attainment of any woman in Washington, and, oh, that it had been given me to know in that my day!"[51]

She appears to have had in the main good health, usually equal to the demands made upon it. When she was ill, she was ill, and gave up: "Always, if sick at all, I am fiercely ill";[52] but she did not like being nursed or cosseted: "To be petted is not my

264

forte." [53] And she had a splendid power of recovery, as she herself puts it: "Recuperativeness, I suppose it is, for I remember an old country doctor telling me, when I was a year older than Flo Gibbs on her birthday, that I had more recuperative power than he had ever seen in any other person." [54] When she was ill and tired, she was sometimes depressed. Sensitive nerves would rebel against the vast burden that was put upon her. Sometimes her husband gently makes fun of her susceptibility, as when, after describing a busy period, he concludes: "Now, wasn't this making the most of day? Had it been you, you would have sat down and cried." [55] Sometimes she herself suggests it directly: "I cannot tell you how dull and stupid I am. I loathe the sight of the Department carriage. Our table is an offense to me. A novel takes on all at once, from the times, a sickly association." [56] But she fought such moods with the persistent energy which is so marked in her, and she urged her children to fight them: "Do not get depressed. It is a family tendency which ought to be put down with a strong hand." [57]

The ordinary external diversions from fatigue and melancholy do not seem to have much appealed to Mrs. Blaine. Now and then she plays a game of cards. She goes to theater and opera and makes shrewd comments. She occasionally buys pictures. But her thoughts were not on such things. When she at length visits Europe, after long desiring it, her attention turns more to people than to places, and she is a number of weeks in Florence before it occurs to her that there is anything to be seen there. Then she sees it dutifully, with the guide-book but I do not gather that the old masters transfigured her life. Even nature, though she often had it about her in its most delightful aspects, hardly gets a word from her. A sunny day cheers her, a dark depresses, but she is usually too busy to notice whether it is dark or not.

Nor does religion figure largely in Mrs. Blaine's brilliant and varied pages. No doubt this was in part owing to a fine and dignified reticence, such as is indicated in her husband's remark as to "those topics of personal religion, concerning which noble natures have an unconquerable reserve." [58] And she had nothing of the rhetoric with which the husband could clothe religion, like everything else, when he saw fit. She was a keen and subtle critic of sermons and preachers; but spiritual emotion does not seem to have often absorbed or transported her. Yet the occasional allusions to it have seriousness and nobility, and in one fine passage of warning to a daughter who seemed likely to come under influences which the mother deplores, she utters a lofty aspiration for spiritual earnestness and independence: "You and I shall find God as easily by our own searchings as the Church has found Him, . . . and I have no sympathies with the cowardice or laziness which has caused so many to acquiesce in the formulas of the Catholic Church. Weariness in well-doing, when nothing seems won, would have stopped every struggle for liberty the world has seen. Millions drop out of the fight, surrendering with a *cui bono*, but the few, the immortal few, who know not how to die nor how to live degraded carry on from age to age the hope of the world." [59]

In her general intellectual life Mrs. Blaine is interesting, suggestive, and active. Busy as she was, she managed to do a great deal of reading, and her comments on it are intelligent. She spends an entire day reading a new novel, and goes to bed "feeling verily guilty. May this lost day never be required of me!" [60] She does not much bother herself with abstract ideas, and metaphysical and scientific theories do not get more than a passing allusion, if even that. But always there is the keen and curious insight, playing with the innumerable incidents and people that throng about her. She will analyze the trial of Guiteau and the love-affairs of a maid in the kitchen with equal penetration and equal profit, well knowing that human nature comes out as much in the one as in the other. She analyzes men and women at large, she analyzes her husband, she analyzes herself, as appears most strikingly from one significant passage, though every page bears more or less the impress of it: "Who came after I know not, every faculty of mine being absorbed in analyzing my feelings." [61] It is this propensity which gives her letters their constant interest. It is this which makes me feel that, in spite of all distractions, she did keep an inner, individual world of her own.

Yet, for all that inner world, it is always evident that her heart and her life were her husband's, bound up with him inseparably. And nothing illustrates this better than the study of the element of ambition in her. Her husband was ambitious, obviously, openly so, though his biographers have tried to belittle this side of him and to maintain that in seeking office he was only doing his public duty. What man who is worth anything is not ambitious? Mrs. Blaine understood him better, and summed him up in the little quotation: "Your father said to me only yesterday, 'I am just like Jamie, when I want a thing, I want it dreadfully.' They are a pair of Jamies." [62] Which reminds one of General

Lee's curious remark about himself, "I am always wanting something." What Lee wanted is not so easy to determine. But it is clear enough that James G. Blaine wanted to be President of the United States.

Only the husband's ambition, though intense, was fitful, and with breaking health it flickered and failed. The wife's was less manifest, she had the stronger and deeper nature, but it was perhaps even more intense and more constant. What her personal hopes and aims may have been in the early separate days before her marriage we do not know. But it is charming to see the gleams of passionate ambition flash out in the dignified restraint and quiet of her letters. There are times when she disclaims it, times when she is weary and wants only quiet and a husband to herself in peace. Then the big world comes back again, the anguish at being fooled of the large part in it which she feels herself so capable of playing. When the nomination is tossed aside against her wishes in 1888, she sighs, "In all my thoughts, which are mostly sympathy for others, I never fail to remember that a nomination is not an election, and that that day of doom has to be lived through." [63] When Guiteau is executed, she murmurs, "Oh, if he only could have died one little year earlier, the difference to

269

me!" [64] Lastly, there is just the brief significant sentence about her daughter's spelling and Mrs. Cleveland: "Feminine Frances is spelled with an 'e.' Think of the first lady in the land, who is not your *chère mère*." [65] What a world of long hopes and blighted ambitions jostle one another in that trivial phrase!

Yet it is evident that all the ambition was inseparable from him. She had no desires, no aspirations that were not intimately connected with his triumph and success. For better, for worse, indeed, for richer, for poorer, her existence was bound up with that of him whom she esteemed "the best man she had ever thoroughly known." And it was through that association that her life became so ample and splendid as it was, so wide and picturesque and intensely varied with joy and sorrow, or as she herself gathers it up in one phrase that condenses the whole, "So much of life and so much love do not often go together." [66]

NOTES

The notes to each chapter are preceded by a list of the most important works referred to, with the abbreviations used.

II. MRS. ABRAHAM LINCOLN

Curtis, William Ellery, *The True Abraham Lincoln.* Curtis.
Herndon, William H., and Jesse W. Weik, *Abraham Lincoln* (edition 1924, unless otherwise specified). Herndon.
Keckley, Elizabeth, *Behind the Scenes.* Keckley.
Lamon, Ward H., *The Life of Abraham Lincoln.* Lamon, *Life.*
Lamon, Ward H., *Recollections of Abraham Lincoln,* Lamon, *Recollections.*
Rankin, Henry B., *Personal Recollections of Abraham Lincoln,* Rankin.
Stephenson, Nathaniel Wright, *Lincoln.* Stephenson.
Tracy, Gilbert A., *Uncollected Letters of Abraham Lincoln.* Tracy.

1. Rankin, p. 121.
2. Rankin, p. 158.
3. *Ibid.*
4. To Marshall, February 8, 1854, Tracy, p. 49.
5. Rankin, p. 122.
6. Recollections of John Hay, Curtis, p. 288.
7. Keckley, p. 181.
8. Herndon, vol. ii, p. 219.
9. William O. Stoddard, *Inside the White House in War Times,* p. 87.
10. Rankin, p. 156.
11. Stephenson, p. 45.
12. To Chambers, 1818, *Letters* (edition Ainger), vol. ii, p. 18.

WIVES

13. Herndon, vol. ii, p. 155.
14. Keckley, p. 101.
15. To Mrs. Keckley, January 12, 1868, Keckley, p. 365.
16. William H. Russell, *My Diary, North and South,* March 28, 1861.
17. George Bancroft to his wife, December 15, 1861. MS. kindly communicated by Mr. Worthington C. Ford.
18. A. Laugel, *Diary,* January 11, 1865, in *Nation,* vol. lxxv, p. 89.
19. Willis Steell, in *Munsey's Magazine,* vol. xl, February, 1909.
20. Curtis, p. 45, authority not given.
21. Keckley, p. 85.
22. To Mrs. Helm, September 20, 1857, Rankin, p. 197.
23. Keckley, p. 149.
24. Vol. ii, p. 137.
25. To Mrs. Keckley, October 6, 1867, Keckley, p. 333.
26. Keckley, p. 104.
27. *Diary of Gideon Welles,* vol. i, p. 325, June 8, 1863.
28. Keckley, p. 182.
29. May 7, 1837, Herndon, vol. i, p. 144.
30. Herndon, vol. i, p. 209.
31. To Marshall, November 11, 1842, Tracy, p. 9.
32. Francis Fisher Browne, *The Every Day Life of Abraham Lincoln* (edition 1913), p. 126.
33. Adam Badeau, *Grant in Peace,* pp. 357-363.
34. William T. Sherman, *Memoirs,* vol. ii, p. 332.
35. Herndon, vol. i, p. 215.
36. Rankin, p. 172.
37. Statement to Herndon, September, 1866, Herndon, vol. ii, p. 223.
38. In Herndon, vol. i, p. 195.
39. Joseph Fort Newton, *Lincoln and Herndon,* p. 18.
40. Herndon, vol. ii, pp. 137, 187.
41. Mrs. Helm, in Rankin, p. 187.

NOTES

42. F. B. Carpenter, *Six Months in the White House with Abraham Lincoln*, p. 302.

43. Herndon, vol. ii, p. 222.

44. Keckley, p. 132.

45. Keckley, p. 133.

46. Keckley, p. 134.

47. Lamon, *Life*, p. 452.

48. Keckley, p. 131.

49. William H. Russell, *My Diary, North and South*, November 3, 1861.

50. Keckley, p. 146.

51. M. A. DeWolfe Howe, *Memories of a Hostess*, p. 189.

52. Lamon, *Recollections*, p. 21.

53. Willis Steell, in *Munsey's Magazine*, February, 1909, vol. xl.

54. *Id.*, p. 623.

55. Dr. Miner, quoted by Reed, as given in William E. Barton, *The Soul of Abraham Lincoln*, p. 334. It is said that the word *Jerusalem* was on Lincoln's lips when the shot was fired; but the anecdote has been filtered through so many heated memories, that it must be regarded with some skepticism.

56. Rankin, p. 181.

57. Stephenson, p. 45.

58. *Ibid.*

59. Herndon, vol. ii, p. 297.

60. Helen Nicolay, *Personal Traits of Abraham Lincoln*, p. 214.

61. It has recently been argued that Lincoln's melancholy had its origin in imperfect digestive processes; but some of us would like to think that spiritual elements entered into it in some measure.

62. Rankin, p. 174.

63. Herndon, vol. i, p. 130, from W. Greene.

64. Mary Owens to Herndon, May 22, 1866, Herndon, vol. i, p. 139.

65. Lincoln to Mrs. M. J. Green, September 22, 1860, Tracy, p. 164.
66. Lincoln to Speed, February 25, 1842, Herndon, vol. i, p. 208.

III. MRS. BENEDICT ARNOLD

Arnold, Isaac N., *The Life of Benedict Arnold, His Patriotism and His Treason.* Arnold.
Walker, Lewis Burd, *Life of Margaret Shippen,* in *Pennsylvania Magazine of History and Biography,* vols. xxiv and xxv. Walker.

1. Walker. vol. xxiv, p. 414.
2. Walker, vol. xxiv, p. 414.
3. To her father, January 5, 1803, Walker, vol. xxv, p. 483.
4. Edward Shippen to his father, December 21, 1778, Walker, vol. xxv, p. 33.
5. Washington Irving, *Life of Washington,* Walker, vol. xxv, p. 148.
6. Manuscript in library of Massachusetts Historical Society, first printed in *My Story: Being the Memoirs of Benedict Arnold,* by F. J. Stimson, p. 333.
7. Arnold, p. 228.
8. Walker, vol. xxv, p. 35.
9. Walker, vol. xxv, p. 36.
10. Walker, vol. xxv, p. 32.
11. S. Weir Mitchell, *Hugh Wynne* (one-volume edition, p. 426).
12. Walker, vol. xxv, p. 40, from Watson's *Annals of Philadelphia.*
13. To Schuyler, Arnold, p. 241.
14. Vol. I, p. 220.
15. J. Parton, *The Life and Times of Aaron Burr* (edition 1858), p. 126.
16. Vol. I, p. 220.

17. In Walker, vol. xxv, p. 149.

18. In Walker, vol. xxv, p. 150. See also *The Varick Court of Inquiry*, by Albert Bushnell Hart.

19. Walker, vol. xxv, p. 155.

20. E. Burd to James Burd, November 10, 1780, Walker, vol. xxv, p. 161.

21. Walker, vol. xxv, p. 155.

22. Matthew L. Davis, *Memoirs of Aaron Burr*, vol. ii, p. 361.

23. Walker, vol. xxv, p. 296.

24. To E. Burd, August 15, 1801, Walker, vol. xxv, p. 474.

25. To her father, January 5, 1803, Walker, vol. xxv, p. 484.

26. March 28, 1802, Walker, vol. xxvi, p. 323.

27. To her father, October 5, 1802, Walker, vol. xxv, p. 480.

28. To her father, March 6, 1786, Walker, vol. xxv, p. 453.

29. Walker, vol. xxv, p. 164.

30. To her father, July, 1792, Walker, vol. xxv, p. 462.

31. To her father, June 2, 1802, Walker, vol. xxv, p. 476.

32. Miss Fitch to Edward Shippen, June 29, 1801, Walker, vol. xxv, p. 472.

33. To her father, January 5, 1803, Walker, vol. xxv, p. 484.

34. March 28, 1802, Walker, vol. xxvi, p. 323.

35. To her sister, July 5, 1790, Walker, vol. xxv, p. 458.

36. To her father, October 5, 1802, Walker, vol. xxv, p. 480.

37. To her father, July 29, 1796, Walker, vol. xxv, p. 466.

38. To her father, January 5, 1803, Walker, vol. xxv, p. 173.

39. To Daniel Coxe, September 17, 1804, Walker, vol. xxvi, p. 330.

40. To her father, July 29, 1796, Walker, vol. xxv, p. 466.

41. Arnold, p. 397.

42. To her father, 1801, Walker, vol. xxv, p. 475.

43. *Ibid.*

44. September 10, 1780, Walker, vol. xxv, p. 43.

45. Walker, vol. xxv, p. 45, from MS. now in Department of State.

46. Walker, vol. xxvi, p. 468.

47. To E. Burd, August 15, 1801, Walker, vol. xxv, p. 177.
48. *Ibid.*
49. To her father, March 6, 1786, Walker, vol. xxv, p. 453.
50. To E. Burd, August 15, 1801, Walker, vol. xxv, p. 473.
51. To Richard Arnold, August, 1794, Walker, vol. xxv, p. 464.
52. To her father, June 26, 1792, Walker, vol. xxv, p. 460.
53. To her father, June 26, 1792, Walker, vol. xxv, p. 462.
54. *Ibid.*
55. To Richard and Henry Arnold, August, 1803, Walker, vol. xxv, p. 489.
56. Arnold, p. 397.

IV. THEODOSIA BURR

Burr, Aaron, *The Private Journal of,* edited by William K. Bixby, two vols. Bixby.
Burr, Aaron, *The Private Journal of,* edited by Matthew L. Davis, two vols. *Journal* (Davis).
Davis, Matthew L., *Memoirs of Aaron Burr,* two vols. *Memoirs* (Davis).

1. *Journal* (Davis), vol. ii, p. 359, March 22, 1812.
2. To her father, December, 1803, *Memoirs,* vol. ii, p. 251.
3. The various rumors as to Theodosia's end are elaborately discussed and analyzed in Charles Felton Pidgin, *Theodosia, the First Gentlewoman of Her Time.*
4. To Burr, August, 1786, *Memoirs,* vol. i, p. 275.
5. December 4, 1791, *Memoirs,* vol. i, p. 308.
6. To Burr, July 27, 1791, *Memoirs,* vol. i, p. 301.
7. To Burr, March 6, 1781, *Memoirs,* vol. i, p. 226.
8. To Mrs. Burr, February 15, 1793, *Memoirs,* vol. i, p. 362.
9. To Theodosia, January 4, 1799, *Memoirs,* vol. i, p. 397.
10. To Theodosia, March 31, 1794, *Memoirs,* vol. i, p. 377.
11. January 16, 1794, *Memoirs,* vol. i, p. 375.
12. August 14, 1794, *Memoirs,* vol. i, p. 382.

NOTES

13. December 4, 1804, *Memoirs,* vol. ii, p. 352.
14. To her father, October 21, 1803, *Memoirs,* vol. ii, p. 243.
15. *Journal* (Davis), vol. i, pp. 114, 241.
16. To her father, November 19, 1803, *Memoirs,* vol. ii, p. 249.
17. July 20, 1803, *Memoirs,* vol. ii, p. 234.
18. Burr to Theodosia, August 4, 1794, *Memoirs,* vol. i, p. 380.
19. Burr to Theodosia, September 17, 1795, *Memoirs,* vol. i, p. 389.
20. Burr to Theodosia, January 4, 1799, *Memoirs,* vol. i, p. 397.
21. William H. Safford, *The Blennerhassett Papers,* p. 469.
22. To Blennerhassett, August 16, 1807, *Id.,* p. 282.
23. See, for example, *Journal* (Davis), vol. i, pp. 75, 76.
24. To her father, May 31, 1809, *Journal* (Davis), vol. i, p. 243.
25. J. Parton, *The Life and Times of Aaron Burr* (edition 1858), p. 626.
26. *Journal* (Davis), vol. ii, p. 430, June 5, 1812.
27. To her husband, August 6, 1805, *Memoirs,* vol. ii, p. 441.
28. Charles Felton Pidgin, *Theodosia, The First Gentlewoman of Her Time,* p. 223.
29. Mrs. Blennerhassett to Blennerhassett, William H. Safford, *The Blennerhassett Papers,* p. 251.
30. Blennerhassett to Alston, March 2, 1811, *Id.,* p. 535.
31. July 10, 1804, *Memoirs,* vol. ii, p. 322.
32. To Theodosia, May 9, 1812, *Journal* (Davis), vol. ii, p. 395.
33. December 28, 1800, *Memoirs,* vol. i, p. 425.
34. February 25, 1813, *Memoirs,* vol. ii, p. 432.
35. June 26, 1802, *Memoirs,* vol. ii, p. 202.
36. September 30, 1802, *Memoirs,* vol. ii, p. 212.
37. October 29, 1803, *Memoirs,* vol. ii, p. 243.
38. See letter of Theodosia to Mrs. Madison, in Charles Felton Pidgin, *Theodosia, The First Gentlewoman of Her Time,* p. 297.

39. To her husband, August 6, 1805, *Memoirs,* vol. ii, p. 441.
40. Burr to Theodosia, April 22, 1809, *Journal* (Davis), vol. i, p. 211.
41. To her father, October 31, 1808, *Journal* (Davis), vol. i, p. 75.
42. To her father, March 17, 1802, *Memoirs,* vol. ii, p. 221.
43. Burr to Alston, March 8, 1802, *Memoirs,* vol. ii, p. 184.
44. To her father, May 31, 1809, *Journal* (Davis), vol. i, p. 240.
45. Bixby, vol. ii, p. 462, June 4, 1812.
46. To Theodosia, April 25, 1804, *Memoirs,* vol. ii, p. 284.
47. To Theodosia, August 8, 1802, *Memoirs,* vol. ii, p. 210.
48. To Theodosia, March 28, 1804, *Memoirs,* vol. ii, p. 282.
49. To Theodosia, May 9, 1812, *Journal* (Davis), vol. ii, p. 395.
50. J. Parton, *The Life and Times of Aaron Burr* (edition 1858), p. 300.
51. To her father, December 10, 1803, *Memoirs,* vol. ii, p. 253.
52. August 12, 1812, *Journal* (Davis), vol. ii, p. 439.
53. To her husband, August 6, 1805, *Memoirs,* vol. ii, p. 441.
54. January 4, 1799, *Memoirs,* vol. i, p. 396.
55. November 21, 1808, *Journal* (Davis), vol. i, p. 100.
56. Bixby, vol. ii, p. 114, January 16, 1811.
57. Bixby, vol. ii, p. 244, September 12, 1811.
58. July 10, 1804, *Memoirs,* vol. ii, p. 322.
59. *Journal* (Davis), vol. i, pp. 77, 242, vol. ii, p. 140.
60. Bixby, vol. ii, p. 9, October 12, 1810.
61. To Jeremy Bentham, January 31, 1809, *Journal* (Davis), vol. i, p. 169.
62. To her father, May 31, 1809, *Journal* (Davis), vol. i, p. 241.
63. October 31, 1808, *Journal* (Davis), vol. i, p. 73.
64. October 13, 1809, *Journal* (Davis), vol. i, p. 317.
65. October 31, 1808, *Journal* (Davis), vol. i, p. 73.

NOTES

66. March 2, 1811, *Blennerhassett Papers,* p. 535.
67. To her father, December 5, 1808, *Journal* (Davis), vol. i,
p. 115.
68. October 31, 1808, *Journal* (Davis), vol. i, p. 77.
69. To her father, October 31, 1808, *Journal* (Davis), vol. i,
p. 72.
70. In Charles Burr Todd, *Life of Colonel Aaron Burr,* p. 133.
71. October 31, 1808, *Journal* (Davis), vol. i, p. 75.
72. August 1, 1809, *Journal* (Davis), vol. i, p. 285.
73. February 1, 1809, *Journal* (Davis), vol. i, p. 160.
74. January 8, 1811, *Journal* (Davis), vol. ii, p. 119.
75. December 6, 1803, *Memoirs,* vol. ii, p. 249.

V. MRS. JAMES MADISON

Goodwin, Maud Wilder, *Dolly Madison.* Goodwin.
Madison, Dolly, *Memoirs and Letters of,* edited by her Grand-
niece. *Memoirs.*
Smith, Mrs. Samuel Harrison, *The First Forty Years of
Washington Society, Portrayed by the Family Letters
of,* edited by Gaillard Hunt. Smith.
1. Mrs. Smith to Mrs. Boyd, August 17, 1828, Smith, p. 234.
2. John Quincy Adams, *Memoirs,* vol. ix, p. 418, October 24,
1837.
3. To Madison, October 28, 1805, *Memoirs,* p. 58.
4. To Dolly Cutts, March 10, 1830, *Memoirs,* p. 178.
5. To Dolly Cutts, November, 1830, *Memoirs,* p. 179.
6. To Mary Cutts, December, 1831, *Memoirs,* p. 183.
7. Goodwin, p. 204.
8. Ticknor to his father, January 21, 1815, George Ticknor,
Life, Letters, and Journals, vol. i, p. 30.
9. To Anna Cutts, June, 1804, *Memoirs,* p. 42.
10. To Mrs. Smith, August 31, 1834, Smith, p. 352.
11. *Memoirs,* p. 15.
12. Pierre M. Irving, *The Life and Letters of Washington
Irving,* vol i, p. 263.

WIVES

13. July 10, 1836, *Memoirs,* p. 200.
14. Goodwin, p. 246.
15. Hunt, in his account of Madison's death (*Life of Madison,* p. 385), disregards this speech, reported by Jennings (*A Colored Man's Reminiscences of James Madison,* p. 20); but it seems to me that the words can hardly have been invented, though there may be question as to the precise moment of their utterance.
16. To Anna Cutts, December 20, 1811, *Memoirs,* p. 73.
17. November 1, 1805, *Memoirs,* p. 60.
18. Quoted from John Quincy Adams, in William Cabell Bruce, *The Life of John Randolph of Roanoke,* vol. i, p. 338.
19. September 16, 1806, *The Writings of James Monroe* (edition Hamilton), vol. iv, p. 487.
20. Quoted in Goodwin, p. 142.
21. The details of this incident have been a matter of dispute. But I think, as I give it, it is well authenticated. See Schouler's *History of the United States,* vol. ii, p. 371, McMaster's *History of the United States,* vol. iv, pp. 82, 83, and Goodwin, pp. 156-158.
22. McMaster, *History,* vol. iv, p. 143, disputes this; but Jennings, *A Colored Man's Reminiscences of James Madison,* p. 10, seems to give good evidence of it.
23. See McMaster, *History,* vol. iv, p. 141, Jennings, p. 15, Goodwin, p. 175.
24. October 23, 1805, *Memoirs,* p. 56.
25. To Mr. and Mrs. Barlow, 1811, *Memoirs,* p. 88.
26. *Memoirs,* p. 208.
27. Mrs. Smith to Mrs. Boyd, August 17, 1828, Smith, p. 237.
28. *Memoirs,* p. 156.
29. Quoted in Goodwin, p. 233.
30. Paul Jennings, *A Colored Man's Reminiscences of James Madison,* p. 17.
31. Gaillard Hunt, *Life of James Madison,* p. 381.

280

NOTES

32. Mrs. Smith's Note-Book, August 4, 1809, Smith, p. 83.
33. p. 19.
34. Laura C. Holloway, *The Ladies of the White House,* p. 178.
35. Paul Jennings, *A Colored Man's Reminiscences of James Madison,* p. 16.
36. Gaillard Hunt, *Life of James Madison,* p. 275.
37. Jennings, p. 16.
38. March 22, 1804, *Memoirs,* p. 46.
39. Gaillard Hunt, *Life of James Madison,* p. 245.
40. Goodwin, p. 208.
41. December 2, 1824, *Memoirs,* p. 167.
42. *Memoirs,* p. 207.
43. *Memoirs,* p. 210.
44. Jefferson to Rush, January 3, 1808, *Works* (Memorial edition, 1903), vol. xi, p. 413.
45. Mrs. Smith's Note-Book, August 4, 1809, Smith, p. 81.
46. To Anna Cutts, July 31, 1805, *Memoirs,* p. 54.
47. Mrs. Smith's Note-Book, August 4, 1809, Smith, p. 81.
48. To Anna Cutts, July 5, 1820, *Memoirs,* p. 173.
49. *Memoirs,* p. 14.
50. *Memoirs of Reverend Dr. John Pierce,* December 23, 1812, in Massachusetts Historical Society, *Proceedings,* Series II, vol. xix, p. 377.
51. Theodosia to her father, in Davis, *Memoirs of Aaron Burr,* vol. ii, p. 242.
52. Laura C. Holloway, *The Ladies of the White House,* p. 200.
53. *Id.,* p. 203.
54. Mrs. Smith to Susan B. Smith, 1809, Smith, p. 62.
55. Seward to Weed, January 24, 1846, Seward's *Autobiography,* vol. i, p. 781.
56. Seward to Weed, January 4, 1846, *Id.,* p. 772.
57. To Susan B. Smith, March, 1809, Smith, p. 62.
58. Paul Jennings, *A Colored Man's Reminiscences of James Madison,* p. 16.

59. Mrs. Smith to Susan B. Smith, March, 1809, Smith, p. 63.
60. *Ibid.*
61. To Anna Cutts, June 3, 1804, Goodwin, p. 47.
62. Paul Jennings, *A Colored Man's Reminiscences of James Madison,* p. 13.
63. To his father, January 21, 1815, George Ticknor, *Life, Letters, and Journals,* vol. i, p. 30.
64. *Memoirs,* p. 84.
65. To Anna Cutts, May 22, 1804, *Memoirs,* p. 46.
66. *Memoirs,* p. 44.
67. Goodwin, p. 73.
68. Laura C. Holloway, *The Ladies of the White House,* p. 177.
69. Philip Hone, *Diary,* vol. ii, p. 121, March 15, 1842.
70. *Memoirs,* p. 209.

VI. MRS. JEFFERSON DAVIS

Butler, Pierce, *Judah P. Benjamin.* Butler, *Benjamin.*
Davis, Jefferson, *A Memoir,* by His Wife. *Memoir.*
Eckenrode, H. J., *Jefferson Davis, President of the South.* Eckenrode.
Pollard, E. A., *The Life of Jefferson Davis.* Pollard, *Davis.*
Roland, Dunbar, *Jefferson Davis, Constitutionalist.* Rowland.
Toombs, Robert, *The Correspondence of Robert Toombs, Alexander H. Stephens, and Howell Cobb,* edited by Ulrich B. Phillips, in *Annual Report of the American Historical Association,* 1911, vol. ii, *Toombs Correspondence.*

1. *Memoir,* vol. i, p. 187.
2. *Memoir,* vol. i, p. 132.
3. Letter in Lawley MS., June 8, 1898, Butler, *Benjamin,* p. 244.
4. Eckenrode, p. 144.
5. *Memoir,* vol. i, pp. 474, 475.
6. To Davis, April 7, 1865, Rowland, vol. vi, p. 539.
7. See *Memoir,* p. 576. A letter preserved in the Confederate

NOTES

Museum at Richmond brings out the circumstances even more vividly.

8. To Mrs. Cobb, October 22, 1868, *Toombs Correspondence,* p. 705.
9. *Diary of Gideon Welles,* vol. i, p. 515. January 26, 1864.
10. To Walthall, September 8, 1878, Rowland, vol. viii, p. 275.
11. April 7, 1865, Rowland, vol. vi, p. 539.
12. Mary Boykin Chesnut, *A Diary from Dixie,* p. 309, May 7, 1864.
13. To Mrs. Cobb, October 22, 1868, *Toombs Correspondence,* p. 705.
14. Senate speech of April 12, 1860, Rowland, vol. iv, p. 231.
15. Eckenrode, p. 291.
16. *Memoir,* vol. ii, p. 498.
17. To Mrs. Chesnut, October 28, 1864, Mary Boykin Chesnut, *A Diary from Dixie,* p. 331.
18. Pollard, *Davis,* p. 154.
19. Morris Schaff, *Jefferson Davis, His Life and Personality,* p. 47.
20. Eckenrode, p. 39.
21. Mrs. D. Giraud Wright, *A Southern Girl in '61,* p. 56.
22. Butler, *Benjamin,* p. 434.
23. Mrs. Roger A. Pryor, *Reminiscences of Peace and War,* p. 81.
24. Pollard, *Davis,* p. 360.
25. *Reminiscences of Rev. W. W. Page.* MS. kindly communicated by Mr. G. Nash Morton.
26. For a most interesting and suggestive analysis of aristocratic conditions and traditions in Virginia before the war see *Virginia Life in Fiction,* Ph.D. thesis by Professor Jay B. Hubbell.
27. Mary Boykin Chesnut, *A Diary from Dixie,* p. 299, March 12, 1864.
28. Mrs. Davis to Mrs. Chesnut, in Mrs. Chesnut's *A Diary from Dixie,* p. 332.

29. *Memoir,* vol. ii, p. 204.
30. To Mrs. Cobb, July 6, 1868, *Toombs Correspondence,* p. 700.
31. *Memoir,* vol. i, p. 164.
32. Pollard, *Davis,* p. 154.
33. John J. Craven, *The Prison Life of Jefferson Davis,* p. 150.
34. Rowland, vol. vi, p. 560.
35. *Id.,* p. 561.
36. *Id.,* p. 562.
37. To Mrs. Cobb, September 9, 1865, *Toombs Correspondence,* p. 667.
38. Beaumont and Fletcher, *The Maid's Tragedy,* act v, scene 4.
39. *Memoir,* vol. ii, p. 71.
40. *Memoir,* vol. i, p. 576.
41. *Memoir,* vol. i, p. 191.
42. *Memoir,* vol. i, p. 199.
43. Memoir, vol. i, p. 178.
44. Butler, *Benjamin,* p. 426.
45. *Memoir,* vol. i, p. 78.
46. *Memoir,* vol. ii, p. 923.
47. MS. in Confederate Museum, Richmond, date probably April, 1865.
48. MS. in Confederate Museum, Richmond, date probably April, 1865.
49. John J. Craven, *The Prison Life of Jefferson Davis,* p. 271.
50. Eckenrode, p. 39.
51. To Davis, Rowland, vol. vi, p. 539.
52. Butler, *Benjamin,* p. 351.
53. Pollard, *Davis,* p. 437.
54. To Davis, Rowland, vol. vi, p. 566.
55. *Examiner,* February 15, 1864, editorial.
56. *Memoir,* vol. i, p. 206.
57. To Davis, April 28, 1865, Rowland, vol. vi, p. 566.

NOTES

58. Elizabeth Keckley, *Behind the Scenes*, p. 71.
59. October 22, 1868, *Toombs Correspondence*, p. 705.

VII. MRS. BENJAMIN F. BUTLER

Butler, Benjamin F., *Butler's Book*. Butler's Book.
Butler, Benjamin F., *Private and Official Correspondence, During the Period of the Civil War*. Correspondence.

1. April 18, 1862, *Correspondence*, vol. i, p. 415.
2. August 8, 1862, *Correspondence*, vol. ii, p. 164.
3. To Mrs. Heard, *Correspondence*, December 10, 1862, vol. ii, p. 530.
4. To Mrs. Heard, April 4, 1862, *Correspondence*, vol. i, p. 403.
5. June, 1864, *Correspondence*, vol. iv, p. 375.
6. To Mrs. Heard, June, 1864, *Correspondence*, vol. iv, p. 338.
7. To Butler, July 16, 1864, *Correspondence*, vol. iv, p. 504.
8. To Butler, August 8, 1862, *Correspondence*, vol. ii, p. 165.
9. To Mrs. Heard, July 6, 1861, *Correspondence*, vol. i, p. 163.
10. June 19, 1864, *Correspondence*, vol. iv, p. 417.
11. To Butler, June 7, 1864, *Correspondence*, vol. iv, p. 323.
12. To Butler, July 19, 1864, *Correspondence*, vol. iv, p. 517.
13. To Butler, October 4, 1864, *Correspondence*, vol. v, p. 221.
14. To Butler, October 9, 1864, *Correspondence*, vol. v, p. 244.
15. *Correspondence*, vol. ii, p. 165, vol. iv, p. 471.
16. To Butler, August 10, 1862, *Correspondence*, vol. ii, p. 175.
17. August 8, 1862, *Correspondence*, vol. ii, p. 164.
18. August 18, 1864, *Correspondence*, vol. v, p. 72.
19. To Butler, August 20, 1864, *Correspondence*, vol. v, p. 84.
20. *Ibid.*
21. To Butler, June 6, 1864, *Correspondence*, vol. iv, p. 319.
22. To Butler, August 15, 1864, *Correspondence*, vol. v, p. 52.
23. To Butler, August 7, 1861, *Correspondence*, vol. i, p. 194.

24. To Mrs. Heard, November 2, 1862, *Correspondence,* vol. i, p. 438.

25. To Butler, August 27, 1864, *Correspondence,* vol. v, p. 115.

26. September 20, 1862, *Correspondence,* vol. ii, p. 317.

27. To Butler, October 5, 1864, *Correspondence,* vol. v, p. 223.

28. To Butler, August 12, 1864, *Correspondence,* vol. v, p. 44.

29. August 27, 1862, *Correspondence,* vol. ii, p. 227.

30. September 14, 1864, *Correspondence,* vol. v, p. 134.

31. September 29, 1862, *Correspondence,* vol. ii, p. 337.

32. Butler to Mrs. Butler, September 13, 1862, *Correspondence,* vol. ii, p. 287.

33. August 22, 1861, *Correspondence,* vol. i, p. 224.

34. August 24, 1864, *Correspondence,* vol. v, p. 108.

35. August 14, 1862, *Correspondence,* vol. ii, p. 190.

36. August 4, 1864, *Correspondence,* vol. iv, p. 596.

37. July, 1864, *Correspondence,* vol. iv, p. 493.

38. September 15, 1864, *Correspondence,* vol. v, p. 137.

39. August 12, 1862, *Correspondence,* vol. ii, p. 186.

40. August 25, 1862, *Correspondence,* vol. ii, p. 218.

41. September 11, 1864, *Correspondence,* vol. v, p. 130.

42. To Butler, August 8, 1862, *Correspondence,* vol. ii, p. 164.

43. June 5, 1864, *Correspondence,* vol. iv, p. 311.

44. June 7, 1864, *Correspondence,* vol. iv, p. 323.

45. To Butler, September 21, 1864, *Correspondence,* vol. v, p. 147.

46. To Butler, August 12, 1864, *Correspondence,* vol. v, p. 45.

47. To Butler, June 6, 1864, *Correspondence,* vol. iv, p. 318.

48. To Mrs. Butler, August 27, 1861, *Correspondence,* vol. i, p. 228.

49. To Mrs. Butler, September 9, 1862, *Correspondence,* vol. ii, p. 272.

50. To Mrs. Butler, September 26, 1864, *Correspondence,* vol. v, p. 170.

NOTES

51. September 29, 1864, *Correspondence,* vol. v, p. 190.
52. To Butler, June 11, 1864, *Correspondence,* vol. iv, p. 342.
53. To Butler, September 28, 1862, *Correspondence,* vol. ii, p. 336.
54. To Butler, June, 1864, *Correspondence,* vol. iv, p. 362.
55. To Butler, July 23, 1864, *Correspondence,* vol. iv, p. 530.
56. *Butler's Book,* p. 82.
57. *Correspondence,* vol. iv, p. 528.
58. To Butler, August 24, 1864, *Correspondence,* vol. v, p. 109.
59. To Butler, June 15, 1864, *Correspondence,* vol. iv, p. 375.
60. To Butler, June 5, 1864, *Correspondence,* vol. iv, p. 311.
61. To Butler, August 18, 1862, *Correspondence,* vol. ii, p. 201.
62. *Butler's Book,* p. 341.
63. To Butler, November 23, 1864, *Correspondence,* vol. v, p. 363.
64. To Mrs. Heard, October 21, 1862, *Correspondence,* vol. ii, p. 393.
65. To Butler, August 8, 1861, *Correspondence,* vol. i, p. 203.
66. June 21, 1864, *Correspondence,* vol. iv, p. 429.
67. July 22, 1864, *Correspondence,* vol. iv, p. 528.
68. To Mrs. Heard, November 28, 1862, *Correspondence,* vol. ii, p. 503.

VIII. MRS. JAMES GILLESPIE BLAINE

Blaine, Mrs. James G., *Letters,* edited by Harriet S. Blaine Beale. *Letters.*
Hamilton, Gail, *Biography of James G. Blaine.* Hamilton.
Stanwood, Edward, *James Gillespie Blaine.* Stanwood.

1. To M., November 28, 1880, *Letters,* vol. i, p. 184.
2. To Emmons Blaine, July 15, 1887, *Letters,* vol. ii, p. 158.
3. To M., March 13, 1883, *Letters,* vol. ii, p. 100.
4. To M., July 6, 1881, *Letters,* vol. i, p. 213.
5. October 29, 1883, *Letters,* vol. ii, p. 110.

6. To Walker Blaine, 1872, *Letters,* vol. i, p. 82.

7. To M., February 21, 1882, *Letters,* vol. i, p. 309.

8. To M., July 3, 1881, *Letters,* vol. i, p. 211.

9. Stanwood, p. 26.

10. To M., June 10, 1881, *Letters,* vol. i, p. 207.

11. To M., March 24, 1882, *Letters,* vol. ii, p. 6.

12. To Alice Blaine, 1862, *Letters,* vol. i, p. 82.

13. To James Blaine, March 5, 1889, *Letters,* vol. ii, p. 250.

14. To Miss Dodge, December 3, 1880, *Letters,* vol. i, p. 185.

15. To Emmons Blaine, November 21, 1879, *Letters,* vol. i, p. 165.

16. To James Blaine, November 12, 1889, *Letters,* vol. ii, p. 281.

17. To M., October 17, 1882, *Letters,* vol. ii, p. 58.

18. To M., December 29, 1881, *Letters,* vol. i, p. 277.

19. To M., March 19, 1883, *Letters,* vol. ii, p. 92.

20. To M., August 14, 1879, *Letters,* vol. i, p. 159.

21. To M., May 13, 1883, *Letters,* vol. ii, p. 101.

22. To M., July 6, 1881, *Letters,* vol. i, p. 212.

23. To M., July 6, 1881, *Letters,* vol. i, p. 214.

24. To Walker Blaine, November 29, 1871, *Letters,* vol. i, p. 66.

25. To Miss Dodge, December 3, 1880, *Letters,* vol. i, p. 185.

26. To M., February, 1883, *Letters,* vol. ii, p. 86.

27. *Letters,* vol. i, preface.

28. To Walker Blaine, December 13, 1881, *Letters,* vol. i, p. 264.

29. To Walker Blaine, December, 1871, *Letters,* vol. i, p. 68.

30. To Miss Dodge, December 3, 1880, *Letters,* vol. i, p. 185.

31. To M., March 19, 1883, *Letters,* vol. ii, p. 92.

32. To James Blaine, February 1, 1889, *Letters,* vol. ii, p. 238.

33. To M., August 14, 1879, *Letters,* vol. i, p. 159.

34. To M., May 8, 1882, *Letters,* vol. ii, p. 16.

35. To M., February 20, 1888, *Letters,* vol. ii, p. 185.

NOTES

36. To Walker Blaine, November 12, 1871, *Letters,* vol. i, p. 56.
37. *Letters,* vol. i, p. 185.
38. Hamilton, p. 455.
39. Hamilton, p. 225.
40. To Walker Blaine, August 18, 1879, *Letters,* vol. i, p. 161.
41. To M., November, 1880, *Letters,* vol. i, p. 179.
42. Harry Thurston Peck, *Twenty Years of the Republic,* p. 288.
43. Hamilton, p. 492.
44. To M., November 2, 1888, *Letters,* vol. ii, p. 218.
45. To M., December 13, 1881, *Letters,* vol. i, p. 263.
46. To M., April 28, 1882, *Letters,* vol. ii, p. 11.
47. To Manley, June 4, 1876, *Letters,* vol. i, p. 136.
48. To Alice Blaine Coppinger, November 30, 1884, *Letters,* vol. 11, p. 120.
49. To Walker Blaine, 1869, *Letters,* vol. i, p. 4.
50. To Walker Blaine, November 12, 1871, Hamilton, p. 263.
51. To M., October 19, 1880, *Letters,* vol. i, p. 175.
52. To M., May 13, 1883, *Letters,* vol. ii, p. 101.
53. To M., January 17, 1881, *Letters,* vol. i, p. 192.
54. To Walker Blaine, November 12, 1871, *Letters,* vol. i, p. 57.
55. Blaine to Mrs. Blaine, July 14, 1878, Hamilton, p. 467.
56. To M., July 25, 1881, *Letters,* vol. i, p. 223.
57. To James Blaine, June 24, 1889, *Letters,* vol. ii, p. 235.
58. R. H. Conwell, *The Life and Public Services of James G Blaine,* p. 392.
59. To M., April 13, 1883, *Letters,* vol. ii, p. 97.
60. To M., September 15, 1885, *Letters,* vol. ii, p. 123.
61. To Walker Blaine, March 12, 1872, *Letters,* vol. i, p. 98.
62. To Emmons Blaine, May 17, 1881, *Letters,* vol. i, p. 201.
63. To Harriet Blaine, February 14, 1888, *Letters,* vol. ii p. 178.
64. To M., June 29, 1882, *Letters,* vol. ii, p. 30.
65. To Harriet Blaine, October 16, 1888, *Letters,* vol. ii, p. 214.
66. To Walker Blaine, May 1, 1872, Hamilton, p. 300.

INDEX

A

Adams, John Quincy, 128, 143, 280

Adams, John Quincy, *Memoirs,* 279

Aladdin, 249, 255

Alert, 138

Alston, Joseph, 92, 102, 103, 104, 105, 106, 107, 110, 119, 277, 278

Alston, Mrs., 99, 111.—*See* Theodosia Burr

American Union, 24

Americans, 82

Amsterdam, 115

André, Major, 58, 63, 69

Aristotle, 104, 105

Arnold, Benedict, 58-63, 65, 70, 71, 74, 78, 80, 82, 83, 85, 86, 87, 88, 276

Arnold, Benedict, My Story: Being the Memoirs of, 274

Arnold, Benedict, The Life of, His Patriotism and His Treason, 274, 275, 276

Arnold, Henry, 276

Arnold, Isaac N., *The Life of Benedict Arnold, His Patriotism and His Treason,* 274, 275, 276

Arnold, Matthew, 234

Arnold, Mrs. Benedict (Mary Shippen), 55-88, 275

Arnold, Richard, 276

Arnold, Sophia, 81

Arthur, President, 240

Augusta, Maine, 237, 246

B

Babes in the Wood, 186

Badeau, Adam, *Grant in Peace,* 36, 272

Bancroft, George, 26, 272

Bar Harbor, 246

Barlow, Mr. and Mrs., 136, 280

Barton, William E., *The Soul of Abraham Lincoln,* 23, 273

Beale, Harriet S. Blaine, 287

Beaumont, *The Maid's Tragedy,* 185, 284

Beauregard, 188

Benjamin, Judah P., 166, 174, 282, 283, 284

Bentham, Jeremy, 278

Biographer, confessions of a, 3-14

Bixby, William K., *The Private Journal of Aaron Burr,* 276, 278

Black Hawk, 165

Blaine, Alice, 243, 257, 288

Blaine, Emmons, 288, 289

Blaine, Harriet, 289

Blaine, James G., 137, 237-239, 245, 247-250, 252-263, 265, 268-270, 288

Blaine, James G., Biography of, 287

Blaine, James G., The Life and Public Services of, 289

Blaine, Mrs. James Gillespie (Harriet Stanwood), 19, 237-270, 287-289

291

INDEX

Craven, John J., *The Prison Life of Jefferson Davis*, 284
Curtis, William Ellery, *The True Abraham Lincoln*, 271, 272
Cutts, Anna, 279, 280, 281, 282
Cutts, Dolly, 279
Cutts, Mary, 279

D

Davis, Jeff, 169
Davis, Jefferson, 23, 164, 165, 170-172, 175, 177, 179, 180-183, 185-190, 192-197
Davis, Jefferson, A Memoir, 282, 283, 284
Davis, Jefferson, Constitutionalist, 282, 284
Davis, Jefferson, His Life and Personality, 283
Davis, Jefferson, President of the South, 282, 283, 284
Davis, Jefferson, The Life of, 282, 283, 284
Davis, Jefferson, The Prison Life of, 284
Davis, Joe, 169
Davis, Matthew L., 64, 65, 69
Davis, Matthew L., *Memoirs of Aaron Burr*, 275, 276, 277, 278, 279, 281
Davis, Matthew L., *The Private Journal of Aaron Burr*, 276, 277, 278, 279
Davis, Mrs. Jefferson (Varina Howell), 163-198, 282-285
Davis, Mrs. Jefferson, *Life* of her husband, 165, 193
Davis, Willie, 169
De Blois, Miss, of Boston, 58-60
Deffand, Madame du, 158
Dickens, Charles, 240
Dickinson, Emily, 244
Dodge, Miss Abigail, 250, 288
Douglas, Stephen Arnold, 85
Dracut, Massachusetts, 201
Dumas, 117

E

Eckenrode, 173, 192
Eckenrode, H. J., *Jefferson Davis, President of the South*, 282, 283, 284
Edwards, Jonathan, 91
Edwards, Matilda, 32, 40
Elkins, Mr., 263
England, 71, 168
English classics, 164
Europe, 108, 116, 144, 266

F

Fields, Mrs., 45
Fisher scandal, 262
Fitch, Miss, 275
Fletcher, *The Maid's Tragedy*, 284
Florence, 266
Ford, Worthington C., 272
Ford's Theater, 47
Fort Stevens, 41
Fortress Monroe, 233
France, Anatole, 132
Franklin, 60
Franks, 66, 70
Fuller, Margaret, 91

G

Garfield, James A., 240, 241, 250, 259, 260, 262
George the Third, 56, 73
Gibbon, 94
Gibbs, Flo, 265
Goncourts, 10
Goodwin, Maud Wilder, *Dolly Madison*, 279, 280, 281, 282
Grant, General Ulysses Simpson, 42, 227, 228
Grant, Mrs. Ulysses Simpson, 205
Grant in Peace, 272
Green, Mrs. M. J., 274
Greene, W., 273
Guerrière, 138

293

INDEX

H

Hamilton, Alexander, 65, 92, 103, 116, 119, 134
Hamilton, Gail.—*See* Miss Abigail Dodge
Hamilton, Gail, *Biography of James G. Blaine*, 287, 289
Hamilton, Lieutenant Paul, 138
Hamlet, 198
Hampton Roads, 194
Hannibal, 123
Harrison, Mrs., 259
Hart, Albert Bushnell, *The Varick Court of Inquiry*, 275
Hay, John, 44, 48
Hay, John, Recollections of, 271
Hay, *History*, 48
Hay's *Diary*, 49
Heard, Mrs., 285, 286, 287
Helm, Mrs., 272
Henry, Joseph, 165
Herndon, Lincoln and, 272
Herndon, William H., 30, 32, 33, 38, 48, 49
Herndon, William H., *Abraham Lincoln*, 271, 272, 273, 274
Herodotus, 94
Holloway, Laura C., *The Ladies of the White House*, 281, 282
Hone, Philip, *Diary*, 282
Hone, Philip, *Journal*, 160
Horatio, 198
Howe, M. A. De Wolfe, *Memories of a Hostess*, 273
Howell, Miss Varina, 164.—*See* Mrs. Jefferson Davis
Howell girls, 176
Hubbell, Professor, Jay B., *Virginia Life in Fiction*, 283
Hunt, Gaillard, *Life of James Madison*, 280, 281

I

Imitation, 51, 151
Ipswich, Massachusetts, 237

Irving, Pierre M., *The Life and Letters of Washington Irving*, 279
Irving, Washington, 102, 133
Irving, Washington, *Life of Washington*, 274
Irving, Washington, *The Life and Letters of*, 279
Ives, 167

J

Jackson, 134, 233
Jefferson, Thomas, 11, 129, 132, 134, 148, 152, 157
Jennings, Paul, 143, 144, 145, 156
Jennings, Paul, *A Colored Man's Reminiscences of James Madison*, 280, 281, 282
Johnston, Joseph E., 167, 188

K

Keckley, Elizabeth, 19, 28, 29, 31, 42, 44, 197
Keckley, Elizabeth, *Behind the Scenes*, 271, 272, 273, 285
Kimball, 227

L

La Rouchefoucauld, 37
Lamb, Charles, 21, 24, 27, 35, 152
Lamon, Ward H., 43, 45
Lamon, Ward H., Recollections of Abraham Lincoln, 271, 273
Lamon, Ward H., *The Life of Abraham Lincoln*, 271, 273
Latin classics, 164
Lauderdale, Lord, 85
Laugel, A., 26
Laugel, A., *Diary*, 272
Lee, General Robert E., 11, 52, 159, 164, 168, 194, 269
Lee, Mrs. Robert E., 176
Letters Aaron Burr, 277, 278; Abraham Lincoln, 274; Benjamin F. Butler, 286; Jeffer-

INDEX

O

Odyssey, 96
Ohio River, 92
Oregon, 44
Owens, Mary, 32, 50, 51, 273

P

Page, Rev. W. W., Reminiscences of, 283
Parton, J., 64, 69, 219
Parton, J., *The Life and Times of Aaron Burr,* 274, 277, 278
Peck, Harry Thurston, 259
Peck, Harry Thurston, *Twenty Years of the Republic,* 289
Pepys, 11, 116
Philadelphia, 55, 57, 62, 71, 83, 128, 164
Philadelphia, Annals of, Watson's, 274
Pidgin, Charles Felton, *Theodosia, the First Gentlewoman of Her Time,* 276, 277
Pierce, Reverend Dr. John, Memoirs of, 281
Plautus, 94
Plutarch, 94
Pollard, E. A., 173, 181, 194
Pollard, E. A., *The Life of Jefferson Davis,* 282, 283, 284
Prevost, Mrs., 93.—*See* Mrs. Aaron Burr
Prevost, Mrs., 64, 65, 67, 69
Pryor, Mrs., Roger A., 174
Pryor, Mrs. Roger A., *Reminiscences of Peace and War,* 283

Q

Quakers, 128, 131, 132, 154
Quintilian, 96

R

Rachel, 66
Randolph, John, 137, 138
Randolph, John, of Roanoke, The Life of, 280

Rankin, Henry B., 20, 36, 38, 48, 50, 272
Rankin, Henry B., *Personal Recollections of Abraham Lincoln,* 43, 271, 272, 273
Renan, 10
Revolution, 56
Richmond, 92, 121, 166, 169, 177, 178
Richmond Examiner, 171, 175, 195, 284
Rickard, Sarah, 32
Ripley, Sarah, 159
"Romance of History," 130
Rowland, Dunbar, *Jefferson Davis, Constitutionalist,* 282, 284
Rush, 281
Russell, William H., 26, 44
Russell, William H., *My Diary, North and South,* 272, 273
Rutledge, Ann, 32, 50

S

Safford, William H., *The Blennerhassett Papers,* 277
Sampson, Dominie, 27
Schaff, General Morris, 171, 173
Schaff, Morris, *Jefferson Davis, His Life and Personality,* 283
Schouler, *History of the United States,* 280
Schuyler, Miss, 65, 274
Sévigné, Madame de, 238, 263
Seward, William Henry, 44, 156, 165, 227
Shakespeare, 201, 222
Shelley, 27
Sherman, General William T., 36, 231
Sherman, William T., *Memoirs,* 272
Shippen, Edward, 56, 76, 78, 79, 274, 275
Shippen, Margaret, Life of, 274, 275
Shippens, 55, 57, 58
Siddons, Mrs., 66

296

INDEX

Smith, Mrs., 143, 151, 153, 156, 157

Smith, Mrs. Samuel Harrison, The First Forty Years of Washington Society, Portrayed by the Family Letters of, 279, 280, 281, 282

Smith, Susan B., 281

Sophocles, 55, 61

South, the, 164, 176, 197, 213, 231

South Carolina, 92, 102, 107, 108, 178

Speed, 34, 39, 52, 274

Springfield, Illinois, 19, 25

St. John's, New Brunswick, 72

Staël, Madame de, 158

Stanton, 41

Stanwood, Edward, *James Gillespie Blaine,* 287, 288

State Rights, 191

Steell, Willis, 46, 272, 273

Stephens, Alexander H., 282

Stephenson, Nathaniel Wright, *Lincoln,* 271, 273

Stephenson, Professor, 23, 49, 171

Stimson, F. J., *My Story: Being the Memoirs of Benedict Arnold,* 274

Stoddard, William O., 23, 30

Stoddard, William O., *Inside the White House in War Times,* 271

Strachey, Mr., 3, 5, 45

Sumner, Charles, 7, 165

T

Tarbell, Ida M., 33

Taylor, Zachary, 180

Terence, 96

Thackeray, 240

Ticknor, George, 131, 158

Ticknor, George, *Life, Letters, and Journals,* 279, 282

Todd, Charles Burr, *Life of Colonel Aaron Burr,* 279

Todd, John, 128, 132

Todd, Mrs., 133

Todd, Payne, 147, 148

Toombs, Robert, 188, 282

Toombs, Correspondence, 282, 283, 284, 285

Touchstone, 21, 35

Tracy, Gilbert A., *Uncollected Letters of Abraham Lincoln,* 271, 274

Twain, Mark, 47

U

Union, 163

United States, 92, 121

Usher, Mrs., 206

V

Varick Court of Inquiry, The, 275

Varicks, 66

Victoria, 45

Voltaire, 11

W

Walker, Lewis Burd, *Life of Margaret Shippen,* 274, 275

Walthall, 283

War of 1812, 134

Washington, D. C., 41, 138, 144, 152, 156, 164, 165, 169, 173, 175, 191, 245, 246, 264

Washington, George, 33, 57, 63, 65, 69, 70, 139, 143

Washington, Life of, 274

Waterloo, 168

Webster, Mr., 146, 165

Weed, 281

Weik, Jesse W., *Abraham Lincoln,* 271, 272, 273, 274

Welles, Gideon, 168

Welles, Gideon, Diary of, 272, 283

West Point, 63, 75, 83, 224

Whigs, 163

White House, 17, 19, 22, 26, 30, 31, 44, 48, 139, 144, 152, 169, 175, 239, 241

INDEX

THE END

American Women: Images and Realities
An Arno Press Collection

[Adams, Charles F., editor]. **Correspondence between John Adams and Mercy Warren Relating to Her "History of the American Revolution," July-August, 1807.** With a new appendix of specimen pages from the **"History."** 1878.

[Arling], Emanie Sachs. **"The Terrible Siren": Victoria Woodhull, (1838-1927).** 1928.

Beard, Mary Ritter. **Woman's Work in Municipalities.** 1915.

Blanc, Madame [Marie Therese de Solms]. **The Condition of Woman in the United States.** 1895.

Bradford, Gamaliel. **Wives.** 1925.

Branagan, Thomas. **The Excellency of the Female Character Vindicated.** 1808.

Breckinridge, Sophonisba P. **Women in the Twentieth Century.** 1933.

Campbell, Helen. **Women Wage-Earners.** 1893.

Coolidge, Mary Roberts. **Why Women Are So.** 1912.

Dall, Caroline H. **The College, the Market, and the Court.** 1867.

[D'Arusmont], Frances Wright. **Life, Letters and Lectures: 1834, 1844.** 1972.

Davis, Almond H. **The Female Preacher, or Memoir of Salome Lincoln.** 1843.

Ellington, George. **The Women of New York.** 1869.

Farnham, Eliza W[oodson]. **Life in Prairie Land.** 1846.

Gage, Matilda Joslyn. **Woman, Church and State.** [1900].

Gilman, Charlotte Perkins. **The Living of Charlotte Perkins Gilman.** 1935.

Groves, Ernest R. **The American Woman.** 1944.

Hale, [Sarah J.] **Manners; or, Happy Homes and Good Society All the Year Round.** 1868.

Higginson, Thomas Wentworth. **Women and the Alphabet.** 1900.

Howe, Julia Ward, editor. **Sex and Education.** 1874.

La Follette, Suzanne. **Concerning Women.** 1926.

Leslie, Eliza . **Miss Leslie's Behaviour Book: A Guide and Manual for Ladies.** 1859.

Livermore, Mary A. **My Story of the War.** 1889.

Logan, Mrs. John A. (Mary S.) **The Part Taken By Women in American History.** 1912.

McGuire, Judith W. (A Lady of Virginia). **Diary of a Southern Refugee, During the War.** 1867.

Mann, Herman . **The Female Review: Life of Deborah Sampson.** 1866.

Meyer, Annie Nathan, editor.**Woman's Work in America.** 1891.

Myerson, Abraham. **The Nervous Housewife.** 1927.

Parsons, Elsie Clews. **The Old-Fashioned Woman.** 1913.

Porter, Sarah Harvey. **The Life and Times of Anne Royall.** 1909.

Pruette, Lorine. **Women and Leisure: A Study of Social Waste.** 1924.

Salmon, Lucy Maynard. **Domestic Service.** 1897.

Sanger, William W. **The History of Prostitution.** 1859.

Smith, Julia E. **Abby Smith and Her Cows.** 1877.

Spencer, Anna Garlin. **Woman's Share in Social Culture.** 1913.

Sprague, William Forrest. **Women and the West.** 1940.

Stanton, Elizabeth Cady. **The Woman's Bible** Parts I and II. 1895/1898.

Stewart, Mrs. Eliza Daniel . **Memories of the Crusade.** 1889.

Todd, John. **Woman's Rights.** 1867. [Dodge, Mary A.] (Gail Hamilton, pseud.) **Woman's Wrongs.** 1868.

Van Rensselaer, Mrs. John King. **The Goede Vrouw of Mana-ha-ta.** 1898.

Velazquez, Loreta Janeta. **The Woman in Battle.** 1876.

Vietor, Agnes C., editor. **A Woman's Quest: The Life of Marie E. Zakrzew-ska, M.D.** 1924.

Woodbury , Helen L. Sumn er. **Equal Suffrage.** 1909.

Young, Ann Eliza. **Wife No. 19.** 1875.